women of
COLOR

Paperback ISBN: 978-1-63616-147-1
eBook ISBN: 978-1-63616-144-0

Published By Opportune Independent Publishing Co.
www.opportunepublishing.com

Printed in the United States of America
For permission requests, email the author with the subject line as "Attention: Permissions Coordinator" to the email address below:
info@opportunepublishing.com

TABLE OF CONTENTS

The Authors of Women of Color

Sharron Terry, Alexis Terry, Shoneika Moore,
Felicia Carroll, Juanika Ballard and
Monica Williams

INTRODUCTION

Colorism, a term defined as "prejudice or discrimination against individuals with a dark skin tone, typically among people of the same ethnic or racial group," has deeply affected the lives of many. In response to the pressing need to address and share personal experiences related to colorism, six remarkable Black women have come together to tell their stories.

Throughout history, disparities in treatment based on skin tone have fueled division among women of color. Lighter-skinned women often found themselves celebrated, while their darker-skinned counterparts faced discrimination, isolation, and harsh judgments. The popularity and acceptance of lighter skin over darker skin have persisted for centuries, creating an environment for division. This issue was compounded when lighter-skinned women sometimes saw themselves as superior to their darker-skinned peers.

It is important to recognize that women, regardless of their skin tone, are resilient and essential contributors to the world. Women, particularly Black women, fulfill an array of roles, from caregivers and homemakers to professionals in various fields. We excel without formal training, juggling multiple responsibilities with grace. Whether one's skin is light, brown, or dark, the brilliance, determination, and fearlessness of Black women are undeniable. Despite the divisive impact of colorism on our culture, we must unite as women first.

Rather than being handpicked or divided, we must stand together as a united force against the divisive power of colorism. We can rise above the shattered remnants of this historical challenge, which has sown discord among us. Black women, as some of the most iconic and influential individuals in history, should not allow colorism to continue dividing us.

It is our collective responsibility to break free from the shackles of colorism and become the embodiment of powerful, unified women, admired and respected worldwide. We invite you to explore our personal journeys as Black women of color, hoping to pave the way for future generations of girls, regardless of their skin tone. Together, we can open doors that reshape history and build a future defined by unity and love.

"Don't ever underestimate the importance you can have because history has shown us that courage can be contagious and hope can take a life of its own."

— Michelle Obama

Felicia Carroll, 61

Felicia Carroll serves as an inspiring figure to many, embodying unwavering determination and a steadfast commitment to self-improvement and community betterment.

With an educational foundation that includes an associate degree in computer science, Felicia has carved a distinguished career path. She currently holds a managerial position at a Travel Management Company, demonstrating her expertise in leadership and organizational acumen.

Beyond her corporate achievements, Felicia is a seasoned entrepreneur, proudly owning and operating "Naturally Beautiful," where she is a Certified Sisterlock Consultant.

Felicia's contributions to her community including advocacy for justice and civil rights earned her the prestigious Dream Keeper's Dr. Martin Luther King Jr. Award—an accolade that reflects her commitment to the timeless truth that "injustice anywhere is a threat to justice everywhere." Furthermore, she actively participates in the Caucus of African American Leaders, further solidifying her commitment to meaningful change and progress.

As a multifaceted individual with a diverse range of accomplishments, Felicia adds the title of "author" to her impressive list of achievements. Her invaluable contribution to a book addressing the critical topic of colorism is a testament to her dedication to addressing important issues and creating a brighter, more inclusive future.

DEDICATION

I wrote this excerpt to encourage and strengthen another brown skinned girl being attacked by her own race. I want her to know that she's enough and that she's beautiful just the way she is and to tell her that the word self in self-esteem means that she should not allow anyone to break her spirit. Please do not allow someone else's insecurities, jealousy and meanness to dim your light.

I would like to thank my mother who always encouraged and loved me though all of the pains and struggles which had been inflicted upon me. You once told me that hurt people, hurt people. At the time, I did not understand it but now I truly understand and appreciate your knowledge and protection.

WHAT IS COLORISM?

I believe it's a manifestation of internalized racism.

As I sit here contemplating the issue of colorism, I find myself wondering when I first became aware of the disdain for the rich, dark hues of my skin within my own community. What I've come to understand is that if you harbor colorist beliefs, it's as if you've internalized self-hate while cherishing a misguided sense of entitlement and acceptance.

I acknowledge that this mindset has its roots in the legacy of slavery and is passed down through learned behavior. What perplexes me is the notion that one's lighter skin somehow makes them superior to those with darker complexions. Have you forgotten that, despite the variations in skin tone, we are all part of the same Black community? Do you not realize that your lighter shade is not a result of privilege, but rather a painful legacy of the trauma inflicted by slave masters? Our ancestors with dark skin were subjected to unspeakable horrors, and their offspring were often denied acknowledgment. How can you justify diminishing, insulting, and humiliating someone with a darker complexion?

So, just because you may have had different circumstances during slavery, such as working in the house rather than the field, does that truly make you superior? Now that I have your attention, let's delve deeper into this important conversation.

THE BEGINNING

Family transcends blood ties; it comprises those who embrace you for who you truly are.

Today, I am a woman with a rich chocolate complexion who came of age during a time when racism was painfully visible. I have both an older sister and a younger brother, all of us sharing the same dark skin, though my brother and I possess the deepest shade. Our parents instilled in us the ideals of Dr. Martin Luther King, envisioning a future where our character, not our skin color, would define us. They presented it as, "White people may judge you, but our own race should stand together." Little did I anticipate that I would one day grapple with internal racism from within our own community.

My deep pigmentation hails from my paternal grandmother's heritage. She was born in 1904, a petite woman with the darkest skin I had ever seen, her white hair concealed beneath a black wig. Later in life, I'd hear people describe her skin as "blue black." To me, her skin was a testament to her rich African heritage, glistening with a natural beauty. My grandmother shared a story from her youth, about someone advising her to use peroxide to lighten her hair. When she did, the peroxide stripped all the pigment from her hair, which never returned to its original black hue. Curious, I asked her why the new hair didn't grow back black, to which she replied, "Baby, I just don't know." I have no memories of my grandmother with black hair; her trademark was that less-than-ideal wig that concealed her white hair.

My mother, on the other hand, was darker than a brown paper bag, yet she didn't possess a dark-skinned complexion. Her challenging upbringing subjected her to teasing due to her clothing, so she ensured that our attire was always fashionable, new, and in line with the latest trends. Our hair received weekly shampooing and straightening. As I write this, I can hear her crooning along to Gladys Knight or Barry White on her albums. She made sure our hair was sleek, silky, and radiant. If our edges reverted due to nighttime perspiration, she'd wield the straightening comb to fix them before we left for school. My mother's care extended beyond our hair; she also made sure we had the trendiest styles. I recall when Jack Purcell sneakers became a trend; we were the first to own them.

Until I reached the age of about eight, my paternal grandparents lived across the street, and my cousins resided next door to them. During school breaks, all our paternal cousins congregated at our grandparents' house while our parents were at work. Back then, my mother was a stay-at-home mom, but we still connected with our cousins. Our neighborhood consisted of three streets: Cooper Road, Scott Avenue, and Henson Avenue, with families we regarded as an extended family. In those days, everyone was addressed as Miss, Mr., Aunt, or Uncle. Adults in the neighborhood could discipline any child verbally, and if they reported it to the parent, the child would face consequences. In this neighborhood, there was no concept of color or shame. We were just children, playing, laughing, and savoring the beauty of life.

We visited my maternal family, and they came to visit us as well. Whether we were maternal or paternal cousins, the distinction didn't matter; we were simply cousins relishing life together. We came in various shades, sizes, and ages, yet none of those differences held any significance.

JAN • 66

THE MOVE

Any change, even a change for the better, is always accompanied by discomforts.

In December of 1970, we bid farewell to our loving and comfortable community, embarking on a new chapter in our lives within a custom-built, single-family home. My parents had achieved their dream of becoming homeowners by acquiring some land. However, the dream was accompanied by a stark reality, as the neighborhood they moved to wasn't a safe place for dark-skinned children. You see, this particular street was home to four houses, all occupied by relatives who either had light complexions or could easily pass the infamous brown paper bag test. It was during this time that I became acutely aware of being perceived as inferior within my own race.

Throughout the school year, we endured daily taunts of being "black and ugly." Name-calling alone wasn't considered bullying in those days, as they termed it "picking" on you. The torment extended beyond words; they held sway over the residents of our neighboring streets. Even individuals with darker skin joined in the name-calling and harassment. At times, they resorted to pushing us on our way to and from the school bus stop, and this torment persisted for years. I found myself compelled to fight back against anyone who laid a hand on either my sister or me. Remarkably, I managed to maintain excellent grades and excelled in mathematics despite the adversity.

During the summer months, the hurtful name-calling would somewhat subside. We had a spacious yard with a swing set and lounge chairs. Occasionally, they were friendly, and my parents allowed them to come over to play. We'd utilize the clothesline as a makeshift volleyball net, and on scorching days, we'd turn on the hose and engage in water play. Why did we play with them, you might wonder? The truth is, we all crave friendship, acceptance, and a sense of belonging within the community. During those moments, it felt like a return to the old neighborhood. Our parents even attended church with one of the families, which fostered a somewhat warmer rapport.

Yet, during quieter moments, I couldn't fathom the reasons behind their animosity. Surely, all this cruelty, animosity, and ugliness couldn't solely stem from the color of our skin. It was about skin color, but it was also about the power they held and the sense of superiority they derived from it. The repercussions of bullying are profound; the isolation it fosters can lead to depression, a lack of acceptance, and, in the most tragic cases, even suicide.

I was oblivious to the fact that my mother, aside from overcompensating for her own difficult childhood, was also compensating for our mistreatment. We'll revisit this later. Little did I know that these experiences would cast a long shadow on my adult life, fostering a sense of low self-esteem.

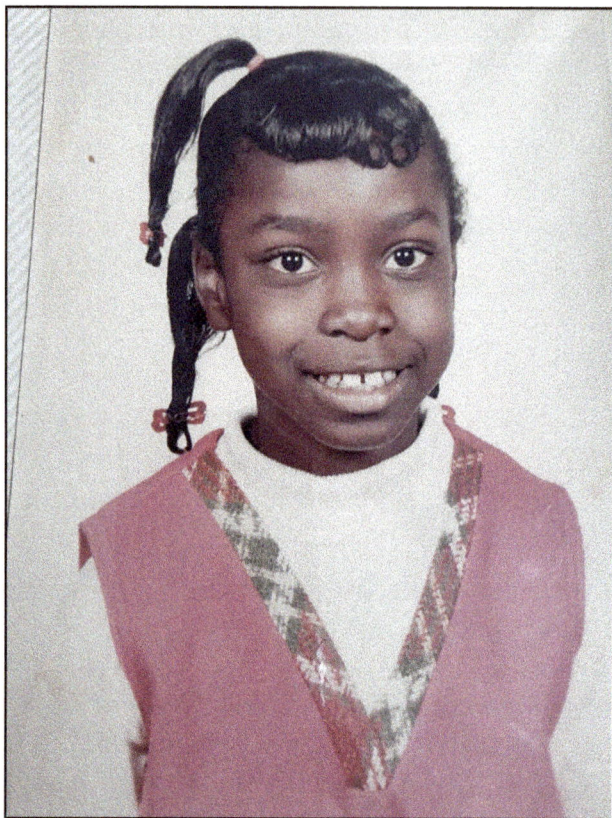

PICK ME

*The greatest gift that you can give to others is the gift
of unconditional love and acceptance.*

As time passed and we grew, our school district changed, and we had the opportunity to meet people from different communities. Although the bullying had ceased, we still carried the emotional scars. The constant name-calling and rejection had deeply affected my spirit, leaving me broken without even realizing it. The societal mindset of favoring light-skinned individuals over dark-skinned ones still prevailed. This made being an adolescent challenging, and dating nearly impossible. Regardless of a light-skinned girl's appearance or body type, she was always preferred.

I remember a song called "Brick House" that emphasized specific measurements as the ideal beauty standard. I measured myself, hoping that my curves in all the right places would give me an advantage. Even if guys were attracted to someone with a darker complexion, they would never openly acknowledge it. During my sixteenth summer, our parents would drop us off at my paternal grandparents' house while they worked. Our cousins had also moved there temporarily, bringing a sense of nostalgia. The female cousins started dating neighborhood guys or the visiting cousins. It was exciting because our skin color was no longer a barrier.

These guys had been crushing on these girls for years. One day, a tall, handsome guy with caramel skin, thick black wavy hair, and a charming smile started talking to me. From that point forward, we talked every day. However, I didn't realize he was also talking to another girl in the neighborhood. She was furious with me because he chose me instead of her. This was a victory for me because she was a light-skinned girl, and I was thrilled that he picked me. However, looking back, I now understand that I was naive to think he was genuinely interested in me. I celebrated my seventeenth birthday in July, and shortly after, we became intimate.

Unfortunately, it only happened once, but I unexpectedly became pregnant. Since my body hadn't regulated its cycle, I didn't realize I was pregnant for around three months. I couldn't help but question what I had done. When I told him about the pregnancy, he rejected both me and our unborn child. While I was pregnant, his family even questioned the paternity of the baby, with concerns about her complexion.

Although he had a light caramel skin color, his family predominantly had lighter skin tones. I prayed for my child to be accepted and to inherit her father's skin color and hair. Looking back, I see how much my prayer revealed about my state of mind.

Now, I realize that I was deeply damaged emotionally. After giving birth, I moved back in with my parents. The colorist neighbors came to see the baby, and although I'm not sure what they expected to see, they spread the word that my daughter was beautiful and light-skinned. This attracted even more visitors.

My daughter grew up with her father's caramel skin and black, curly hair. We continued to have an on-and-off relationship until she turned three. During one visit, I overheard his sisters discussing my complexion, and how they were relieved that their niece was beautiful.

I kept my feelings to myself and pretended not to hear their hurtful comments. Deep down, I was glad that my child would not have to endure the same experiences I did.

Unfortunately, my pattern of making poor choices in dating continued. I would date men who were interested in me, but I never considered what I wanted in a person or a relationship for myself. I often found myself dating men who were at least six feet tall and slim. However, at the age of 49, a friend introduced me to a guy who wasn't my usual type. I realized that I had been consistently dating the same type without any success, so I gave him a chance. He was about 5 feet 8 inches tall and had a stocky build. He treated me well, and everything seemed to be going smoothly. I thought that finally, someone saw me for who I was. However, after four months, his behavior changed, and I could sense that something was wrong. When I asked him about it, he claimed everything was fine, but deep down, I knew things had shifted.

Eventually, he admitted that I had all the qualities he was looking for except for one thing: my complexion. What was even more disheartening was that his mother, whom he loved dearly, had a darker complexion than mine. Within two months, he attempted to reconcile, but I declined. He continuously tried for almost a year, sending calls or texts every few months, apologizing for his ignorance. However, I could never trust him with my heart again. It was a cycle of feeling unworthy, not pretty enough, and constantly being told that I was "cute for a dark-skinned girl."

I can't even begin to count the number of times I've heard that comment. In preparation for writing about my experiences as a dark-skinned person, I confided in a light-skinned girl about being tired of hearing that phrase. She couldn't believe people would say such things to me. I understood the intention behind her statement. She wanted to highlight that I was not just "cute for a dark-skinned girl."

At the time, I was 59 years old, but internally, I still felt the pain of that nine-year-old girl. I had learned not to react angrily, but I also hadn't confronted the issue. Why? It was for the same reason I allowed people to mistreat me and still came back to play with my toys. It was the same reason I let men choose me without having a voice to say that I didn't actually care about them or their feelings. It was because I didn't love or respect myself, nor did I appreciate the beauty I possessed both inside and out.

SEEKING HELP

"Counseling has to do with intuition, with work on oneself, with the quietness of one's mind and the openness of one's heart." —Ram Dass

L ife as a person with a darker skin tone was a continuous challenge. Everywhere I went, it seemed to reflect my childhood experiences, serving as a constant reminder of my perceived inadequacy. Even after I graduated from high school and pursued a college education, earning a degree in computer science, my intelligence and accomplishments failed to alleviate my feelings of self-doubt.

I mentioned earlier how my mother had instilled in me the importance of immaculate clothing and flawless hair. I carried on that tradition with my own children. While they had skin darker than a brown paper bag, I still went to great lengths to ensure they wouldn't face bullying.

Nearly three decades ago, seeking counseling openly was not common among African Americans, but I realized that I needed help to navigate my emotions, build my self-esteem, and learn to love myself. I delved into self-help books, which offered valuable advice, yet I struggled to consistently uplift myself. I came to realize that I was merely existing, not truly living. At the age of 31, I decided to seek professional counseling. During my therapy sessions, I was challenged to delve into our history.

"Dark skin is a stigma. It dehumanizes you." – Viola

Davis

The dehumanization of dark skin is so pervasive that darker-skinned individuals resort to skin-lightening techniques to escape mistreatment, despite the known health risks. While researching my history, I discovered many unsettling facts. For instance, teachers often treated lighter-skinned children more favorably than their darker-skinned peers. Light-skinned individuals would seek relationships and have children with others of a similar complexion to preserve their lineage, avoiding the birth of a darker-skinned child. Segregation existed within our own community.

We often discuss the harm inflicted upon African Americans by Caucasians, but we seldom acknowledge the damage we've inflicted upon one another. This reality doesn't diminish the lasting effects of slavery in our community. When I reflect on the struggle for equality, I find it challenging to comprehend how we could mistreat each other.

The truth of the matter is that the name-calling, belittling, and bullying were not about the dark-skinned person. They stemmed from the internal struggles of those with lighter skin. So, where do we go from here? How can we address this internal racism?

Sharron Terry, 55

Sharron Terry is a Licensed Professional Counselor Associate in Texas and founder of Purple Reign Counseling and Consulting, PLLC. She has a Master of Science in Mental Health Counseling and is a National Certified Counselor. She is also a Certified Grief Counselor.

She knows how challenging life can be. Sometimes, even the strongest people need help to work through some of life's tougher problems. Everyone has battles to fight and hurdles to overcome at some point. Whether the struggle is with anxiety, depression, self-esteem, grief, substance abuse, or any other issue, there is hope for a better tomorrow. It is okay not to be okay.

She is passionate about providing a safe place for women who are there for everyone but feel they have no one to be there for them. She considers herself their champion because she was them. She works with women from all walks of life to navigate challenges by learning healthier coping skills, starting with self-love.

She lives in Texas with her husband and loves spending time with her sons and grandchildren, whom she adores. Sharron finds joy in traveling with family and friends.

DEDICATION

To my granddaughters, always remember that God knows his plans for you, "plans to prosper you and not to harm you, plans to give you hope and a future," (Jeremiah 29:11). You are perfect in my eyes.

To my beautiful brown sisters, when you learn to love yourselves first, it won't matter who doesn't. You're more than enough.

CONNECT WITH SHARRON

Purple Reign Counseling and Consulting, PLLC:
Website https://purplereigncounseling.com/
Email: info@purplereigncounseling.com
FB: @purplereigncounseling.com
Twitter: https://twitter.com/purplereigntalk

BROWN PAPER BAG TEST

"Distinguishing color – light, black, in between – as the marker for race is really an error: It's socially constructed, it's culturally enforced and it has some advantages for certain people. But this is really skin privilege – the ranking of color in terms of its closeness to white people or white-skinned people and its devaluation according to how dark one is and the impact that has on people who are dedicated to the privileges of certain levels of skin color."
—Toni Morrison

"The **Brown Paper Bag Test**" is a term used to describe discriminatory practices within the Black community, in which an individual's skin tone got compared to the color of a brown paper bag. If you were the color of the brown bag or lighter, admission was granted to social clubs, sororities, employment, and other benefits. However, if you were darker, you were denied access or treated like an alien from another planet.

BROWN BAGGIN IT

Look ma, I passed the brown bag test. I can get in where I
fit in.
I am neither light bright nor dark as night.
I am neither Becky with the Good Hair or a Black Queen, so
I don't care.
I am Brown like the dirt of the earth, necessary like the air.
You measured my worth by the color of a brown bag.
I find that to be sad.
My own kind, my so-called sisters, consider me too basic.
The bare minimum of our culture which makes mad.
My brown skin is more than a brown paper bag.
Yes, I was created to carry burdens that I never should
have.
Yes, I can break when the weight is too great and
Yes, one day this flesh of mine will disintegrate and I will
return to dust.
Until then...I will celebrate this beautiful brown skin I live
in.
Until then...I will peel back the layers of she who is me.
My brown epidermis is my protection from the infection of
this so-called selection.
Hmph. Light skin burns quickly while dark skin burns
slowly. Neither respect the Son.
Or accept that we are many members of ONE.
The layer you cannot see is my dermis which cools me

amid this chaos.
Can't you see that this colorism – brown bag thing is a farce?
Will you look deeper to see what lies within the last layer of my skin?
Subcutis. It warms and protects my heart from turning to ice when my brown skin just will not suffice.
You will find there is still love there. Even if you will not accept my kinky hair.
You will find forgiveness. Even if you do not want it or even care.
It is for me, but I am willing to share.
You see. I have thrown away that brown bag.
I refuse to be in a place that will not embrace all shades.
I am in a place where I am free to be me.
Look ma, I have created my own stage.

BOYS MAKE GIRLS GO CRAZY

*"The deepest of a woman's insecurities often come
from the men who have hurt them."*
—Egypt-Thegoodvibe.co

I grew up in a family of mixed hues, maternal and paternal. I do not recall any of us being put down because of our skin tones. My story is unlike others because I am neither light nor dark brown. I refer to myself as light brown sugar with skin smooth as butter. "You're so pretty." "She's beautiful." I passed the brown paper bag test, which granted me acceptance until I became a teenager.

Boys make girls go crazy. I can only remember one major incident where my beautiful brown skin got me into trouble. Middle school, 7th grade. I was in the backyard, hanging clothes and minding my own business, when some high school girls who lived across the street walked by and called me a bitch. At first, I thought they were yelling at someone else because I had nothing to do with them. One of the girls started spewing threats at me. "I'm going to beat your ass after school tomorrow."

The next thing I knew, I heard knocks at the front door with the news. (Let's call my nemesis-Ladybug). "Ladybug said she's going to get you."

"What did you do?"

"She said you called her a bitch."

I was dumbfounded because she completely flipped

the script and convinced everyone that Trina (my nickname) was a she-devil dressed in sheep's clothing. Sure enough, as my bus pulled up to the stop the next day, I saw Ladybug and her high school entourage waiting for me. Butterflies took over my stomach. My mind was racing. *Will I be fighting only her, or am I about to be jumped?* I had only been in one other fight in my whole twelve years of living. I knew that I could fight because of what happened in my first fight, but I was nervous because many high schoolers were waiting for me. When my feet touched the ground, I was in it to win it. My blood boiled as I entered the blackout zone. The next thing I knew I was walking into my mother's house and grabbing her Princess House crystal wine decanter. Of course, my mother did not let that get past her, which left me no choice but to get a giant stick I could find to finish the job. She started it, and I was prepared to finish it. Fortunately, my high school friends intervened, and from what I heard, they threatened her and told her never to bother me again.

Eventually, the truth came out. Ladybug was a darker shade than me, and evidently, she was jealous because of her boyfriend. Remember that I'm twelve, and they were both in high school. I had no interest in him because I was seriously saving myself for Prince. He must have commented on my looks, or she heard him say something to someone. The bottom line is that I had done nothing wrong, and she projected her insecurities onto me. Ladybug thought I was better than her. However, it was easier for her to say that I thought I was better than her. Little did she know I struggled with wanting to be liked. Colorism.

As I got older, I learned that most guys wanted "Redbones" with long hair, large breasts, and butts. I lacked in all those areas. Ironically, I had no desire for them. Jealousy was something that escaped me. As I reflected on the situation with Ladybug and others accusing me of being high-minded (people who didn't know me), I started downplaying my beauty and shape to make others comfortable. I have never thought that I was better than anyone or that anyone was better than me because of the shade of their skin. There are plenty of ugly people clothed in beautiful skin.

Black women experience colorism at exponentially higher rates than black men, referred to as "gendered colorism" (Hill, 2002: 77-91). I have heard black men boast about using light-skinned women as trophies on their arms, particularly in politics and business. *The Color Purple* (1985) depicts the disparity of treatment between Shug and Ms. Celie. He loved Shug and became excited whenever she was around. Her "love him and leave him" attitude toward him was accepted and welcomed. Meanwhile, he abused Ms. Celie by calling her derogatory names, using her "to do his business", and be his maid. In the documentary *Dark Girls 2* (2020), dark-skinned women were accused of being troublemakers or "haters" when speaking up for themselves while their lighter counterparts were celebrated. Women from Africa shared that men preferred lighter women so that they could still see them in the dark while in bed. Unbelievable. Viola Davis said, "It is a widely held belief that dark-skinned women just don't do it for a lot of Black men. It's a mentality rooted in both racism and misogyny, that you have no value as a woman if you do not turn them on, if you are not desirable to them. It's ingrained thinking, dictated by oppression" (*Finding Me, 2022*)

According to Nielsen, black women spend about 7.5 billion dollars annually on beauty products (EmilyReuman, 2023). Women compete against other women of color, not to mention trying to become the standard of a white woman. We straighten our hair, lighten our skin, and lighten our eyes with contacts. Front lace wigs have replaced natural hair. Women who dare to be natural are criticized or are less desirable. White women spend millions of dollars on tanning and implants to enlarge their breasts and butts. Botox is used to create fuller lips. We are destroying each other's sense of self-worth. We are losing ourselves. I lost myself by attempting to become less threatening to other black women.

IMPACT ON MENTAL HEALTH

*"Not everything that is faced can be changed; but
nothing can be changed until it is faced."*
—*James Baldwin*

One day the dam broke, evident by tears rolling down my
face as I stood there staring at this stranger in the mirror.
During that time, my life was dedicated to my God, husband,
children, church, and work. I reached a breaking point because
even the church made me smaller. The women, particularly
the church's mothers, told me I should not wear short hair.
I loved short haircuts. I found myself wearing longer and
longer skirts. As a leader of the church, I saw way too much.
Colorism, amongst other isms, was in full play. Deacons
were sure to "hug their neighbors" tighter than some others.
Women were constantly competing for male attention in
Jesus' Name. Light-skin or exotic-looking women seemingly
had the first pick. Fortunately, I was already married.

I mention church because it is the cornerstone of the
Black community and should be where we find refuge, comfort,
spiritual meaning, hope, and encouragement. Those things
were present, but it became a two-edged sword. Although the
Black congregation consisted of 70 to 90% women (Thomas,
2016), the church became another male-dominated place
where women were subservient and competed. Big hats and
fancy suits separated the wheat from the tare.

After talking with Jesus, I traded where I served for

a non-denominational church full of progressive people. The women were welcoming without pretenses. Initially, I struggled to wear pants for fear of being reprimanded and judged by the female elders and women in general. It was refreshing because it felt like like-minded women surrounded me. As mentioned, I have never been jealous-hearted or in competition with my brown sisters. I want us all to win; these women wanted the same thing.

I remember attending my first conference at the new church. The leaders of the women's ministry challenged us to show up as our authentic selves. Make-up removers were provided for those who did not get the memo. We were all given mini mirrors to look at ourselves without the condemning voices of others or ourselves. Healing profoundly began for me. I saw myself again in plain view. A woman who loved to wear light make-up, jeans, and T-shirts. A woman who loved sitting by the water, particularly a beach or a lake while listening to Gospel and R&B. The women there saw me and embraced my beautiful brown skin, and I embraced all their shades, from light to dark and everything in between. We were not in competition with our White or Latina sisters either. It was pure love and acceptance. Women need women because iron sharpens iron.

Colorism fosters isolation, self-hate, and self-rejection. How can we love others if we hate ourselves? Love starts with ME loving ME. As I became smaller, my resentment grew stronger toward other women, but I still tried to conceal it because everyone had to be comfortable but me. People pleasing became exhausting. Feeling like I was under a microscope was exhausting. The more I gave, the more people wanted from me. I gave and gave until there was nothing left. Not even for me.

As a result, burnout, and depression crept in. Some would say I became the stereotypical angry black woman. However, very few took the time to consider why I responded the way I did. Fortunately, my inner circle of friends was there for me. We understood each other and provided support. We still do... thirty-plus years and counting. At this point, they are my sisters from another mother and quite honestly, I need them. Women who do not have a strong support system are at risk for substance abuse, self-injury, risky sexual behavior, and increased anxiety. As a therapist, I help women find themselves as they began their journeys to self-love. Many of them, like me, never asked themselves the question: What do I need? What do I want? What will make me happy? What parts of me can I afford to give away and what parts are reserved for only me?

TIME TO HEAL

"When a deep injury is done to us, we never heal until we forgive." —Nelson Mandela

How can we heal this traumatic divide perpetuated throughout generations of Black people or African Americans (if you prefer)? It must start somewhere. It must begin with you and me today! Our future generations of brown girls do not deserve to be traumatized as we have been. My granddaughters deserve better, mainly because we know better. As Maya Angelou would say, "When you know better, you do better."

To heal personally, I began by replacing all negative self-talk with positive self-talk. In most cases, we did not realize anything was wrong with us until someone told us their thoughts. I wrote positive affirmations on sticky notes and put them all around my mirror. Whenever negative thinking tried to enter my mind, I battled it with positive affirmations. It may be hard to convince yourself that the claims are valid. You may feel like you are lying to yourself. Think of it this way; you have been telling yourself bad lies for so long, replace them with good lies until they become your truth.

Learning to say no to others and say yes to myself was an excruciating process. However, in doing so, I quickly learned who genuinely wanted to be in a relationship with me for who I was and not what I could do for them. I forgave myself for allowing others to treat me poorly and vowed to do better no matter who it was. The road to self-awareness and self-love was not easy but it was worth the struggle. Today, I am intentional about how I show up for myself and others.

Remember, you did not start colorism, but you can end it whether you are the giver or receiver. Colorism was birthed out of racism to divide and conquer. We need to accept what others already know. We are a mighty nation of queens and princesses who are powerful when united.

It is okay not to be okay. Reach out to your friends and family who provide a safe, non-judgmental place for you. If you are uncomfortable with being vulnerable to them, seek professional help. I promise you; a therapist will not bite. I will admit that sometimes finding a therapist is like trying on shoes. You may have to try some of them out before finding the right fit. Even as a therapist, I have had therapists. Our families taught, "What goes on in this house...stays in this house?" Well, it is clear to see where that has gotten our culture. We do not have to suffer alone or in silence anymore. It is time to heal from all the aftermath of colorism, amongst other traumas.

What if you were the mean light, brown, or dark girl? How can you move forward? Begin with self-forgiveness and compassion. Then proceed to forsake harmful language directed toward other people of color. Affirm, uplift, and celebrate other women. Practice giving random compliments. If you have nothing positive to say, do not say anything until you do.

Acknowledge your privilege if your skin tone has granted you access to people, places, and things. Denial of this privilege diminishes other women's experiences of their treatment caused by your privilege. I know there have been times when my looks allowed me to experience things I would not have if I were darker.

When possible, apologize to whomever you have offended or intentionally harmed. If it is impossible, make amends by intentionally treating your sisters of all shades with respect and positive regard. Also, ask questions instead of making assumptions. Everything is not always as it appears to be. Generally, I give people the benefit of doubt. My husband refers to me as "the public defender". I listen to understand not to respond. I try to imagine what it would be like to walk a mile in another woman's shoes. For example, I imagine how challenging it would be for a woman of a darker shade who is ostracized or viewed negatively for something that she cannot change...the color of her skin. Marginalization within her own culture and society as a whole is devastating to her soul.

GOOD,
GOOD GIRL FRIEND TIME

*"We should always have three friends in our lives-
one who walks ahead who we look up to and follow;
one who walks beside us, who is with us every step
of our journey; and then, one who we reach back for
and bring along after we've cleared the way."*
—Michelle Obama

One of my favorite things to do is spend quality time
with my good, good girlfriends. We have had some epic
vacations, dinners, parties, and events. We ordered food and
sipped wine as we whined in one of our living rooms. By the
way, brown paper bags with food and drinks are permissible.
We give life to each other, and I miss them when time lapses.
There are times when we agree to disagree, and that is fine by
me. I love the female energy. Research shows that spending
time with other women can reduce stress, improve overall
mental, and physical health. I know this to be true because I
have experienced the palpable love of a sisterhood who has
provided support through illnesses, failed relationships, and
the challenges of raising boys to men in America (which is a
book of its own). Through it all, I am reminded we are fearfully
and wonderfully made in different shades.

Monica Williams, 51

Monica Williams is a renowned speaker, celebrated for her ability to inspire, motivate, and educate women with messages of hope and resilience. She is the visionary and founder of "Women of Truth," a women's group established in 2014. Monica's passion lies in empowering women, dismantling the barriers of their past, and fostering an environment of authenticity and growth.

With a profound commitment to her mission, Monica

walks the path of strength and humility, making her a formidable force for positive change. She provides a secure platform where women can embrace their true selves, free from the weight of their past mistakes, enabling them to step boldly into the world as authentic individuals.

Monica's influence extends far and wide, as she has had the privilege of speaking at various prestigious events, including her Alma Mater, Millersville University, live social media gatherings, middle schools, residential homes for youth, and esteemed panels such as the Wa Na Wari Panel Discussion during the Urban Book Expo in Seattle, Washington, and DC Black Pride at Literary Café.

In addition to her impactful speaking engagements, Monica is a published author. Her debut book, *How I Loved GOD and Her: The Battle of the Heart*, garnered recognition in the *York Dispatch* newspaper. Her second book, *The Unveiling: Pain, Trauma & Truth*, published in 2022, achieved remarkable success, repeatedly ranking in the top 100 on Amazon New Releases and in the Sociology of Abuse category. She also co-authored *Baldness with Boldness: Unmasking Alopecia, Revealing Resilience.*

Monica holds an Associate of Arts degree in Social Sciences from Harrisburg Area Community College. In 2014, she earned a Bachelor of Arts degree from Millersville University, graduating cum laude. Monica furthered her education by obtaining a Master of Social Work degree in 2016, graduating with honors and a perfect 4.0 GPA from a dual college program at Shippensburg and Millersville Universities. Her academic excellence earned her induction into the Theta Alpha Phi Alpha Honor Society.

Currently, Monica thrives in her career as a medical social worker, offering end-of-life support to hospice patients and their families.

Monica's personal life is equally fulfilling. She shares her life with her spouse, Juanika Ballard, and together they are proud parents to twins, adding to their family of five children from previous relationships. They reside in York, Pennsylvania, where they relish in family vacations, quality time, creating lasting memories, and cherishing each moment. Together, they affirm, "We are living our best life, but the best is yet to come."

Monica Williams is not only a source of inspiration but also a beacon of hope and positivity in her community and beyond.

ACKNOWLEDGMENT

I would like to thank God for giving me the desire and vision of the *Women of Color* project and for giving me the courage to not quit when I wanted to many times. I want to thank my late mother, Jeanette Wilkins (9-23-1996), for birthing me and teaching me how to survive. I want to praise my late grandmother, Anna Wilkins (2-8-1978), for taking the time to be selfless enough to care for me until she died. I want to honor my aunt Wilma Carter for always having a positive influence in my life and teaching me impactful lessons that shaped me into becoming the woman I am today. *THE GREATEST WOMEN OF ALL TIME*!!

I would like to give the BIGGEST thank you to my spouse and best friend, Juanika Ballard, who so graciously accepted being a part of this team of incredible Black women. I want to thank her for loving me as I was and as I am now. I want to thank her for always supporting me on every journey in life and always encouraging me to do better than my best. *I LOVE YOU BEYOND WORDS*!!

I would like to thank my five children, Anthony, Demetrick, Kenji, Sohn and Surae for giving me purpose to strive and thrive, and helping me to keep my head up when holding it down felt safe. Thank you all for being my five heartbeats. I would like to thank my two grandchildren, Khamil and Ace, for bringing so much joy into my world. I LOVE ALL OF YOU *DEEPLY*!!

I would like to thank all of my wonderful and supportive sister friends who pray for me, encourage me, inspire me, love me and motivate me when I'm up and down. Thank you all for showing up for me through the good and bad times. I love looking up and seeing all of your beautiful faces; I could not ask for a better circle of friends. SISTER FRIENDS FOR LIFE!!

I would like to thank my sisters, Danielle and Tara; my brother, Andre; cousins Kia, Trina, and late cousin Melvin (10-18-2011); and all my extended family for the love and continued support. You all are the best—ever—and there is nothing I would not do for each of you. Thank you all for always believing in my dreams and aspirations. FAMILY MATTERS!!

I would finally like to thank the women behind the scenes whose stories you will have the honor of reading. Thank you again, Alexis, Felicia, Juanika, Sharron (Trina) and Shoneika for saying YES!! You ladies are ROCKSTARS, and I love each of you in a special way! *WOMEN OF COLOR UNLEASHED*!!

"The idea is to write it so that people hear it and it slides through the brain and goes straight to the heart."
— Maya Angelou

DEDICATION

These *Women of Color* stories are dedicated to every Black and brown woman who has negatively experienced colorism. At some point in our lives, we have been marginalized by a system or organization of some sort that discredited us based on our skin color. Colorism has plagued women for decades, causing insecurities, depression and inadequacies. In addition, it has impacted mental health issues, which made us question our true identity as Black women surrounding this problem.

Thank you to all the amazing Black women who stood through the test of times and didn't give up when everything proved you should have. Thank you to all the revolutionary women who paved the way and have gone unnoticed. We have seen your iconic sacrifices and your determination to make a monumental difference in this world. Thank you to every Black woman who linked arms during times of shame when your voices were silenced. Thank you for your examples that helped forge a path for many women after you to be great.

Thank you to all our Black empowered queens, boss chicks, CEO s, entrepreneurs, college graduates and working women who are climbing the ladder of success. We are doing what was never expected: moving mountains and breaking barriers. Thank you for showing up in a world that tries to hide us in the background. Thank you for sharing your awesome Black and brown selves and for being seen. Malala Yousafzai said, "I tell my story not because it is unique, but because it is the story of many girls."

CONNECT WITH MONICA

Website: www.womenoftruthco.com
Email: Monica.williams0313@gmail.com
Facebook: Monica Williams Published Author

THE IDENTITY OF MY BLACKNESS

James Brown said it best:
"'I'm Black and I'm proud'
Say it louder (I'm Black and I'm proud)
Say it louder (I'm Black and I'm proud)
One more time, say it loud (I'm Black and I'm proud)
Say it again, 'I'm Black and I'm proud!'"

I am BLACK, PROUD, and RELENTLESS! Indeed, that's who I am. I've been resolute in my determination, persisting through every obstacle, unwavering in my struggles, steady in my steps and journey, relentless in my battles, and unshakeable in my pursuit of becoming the proud woman of color I am today.

I remained strong in moments of weakness, found hope when life threw me down, smiled through life's storms, conquered tests, trials, and tribulations, surmounted mountains, navigated through trust and doubt, held my head high in the face of defeat, and prayed my way through troubles. Yet, I remained a resolute woman of color. I've experienced loss and gain, moments of despair and triumph, homelessness and shelter, hunger and fulfillment, financial hardship and mending, rejection and acceptance, abandonment and love, confusion and certainty. Nevertheless, I stood strong as a woman who endured the challenges of life, never faltering.

Yes, that's ME—Proud and resolute, unapologetically BLACK!

TRUTH BE TOLD

*"Honesty is more than not lying. It is truth telling,
truth speaking, truth living, and truth loving."*
— *James E. Faust*

Race has long been a complex issue for women of color, particularly for those in the Black and brown communities. Questions about my place within the Black community based on the shade of my skin have always lingered. My formative years in the '70s and '80s were predominantly spent among Black peers, rarely encountering other ethnic groups. Oddly, my skin tone held more significance for others than it did for me.

In the early '80s, due to family circumstances, I found myself living with a family friend—who was living with a white family himself. The experience felt different, not so much due to the obvious differences but because we didn't share the same skin color, which felt bewildering. However, as a 10-year-old, I couldn't articulate these thoughts, and my understanding of racial differences was limited. All I knew was the distinction between light and dark, shaped by the preconceived notions of others, associating lighter skin with beauty and privilege.

At that time, I couldn't reconcile the idea of being a Black woman with my light skin. I used to insist that I wasn't Black; I was "light-skinned." The real question was whether I would acknowledge my Black identity or continue denying a significant part of who I am. It was high time to reevaluate my stance. My Blackness was intrinsic, always a part of me. The connection was unbreakable, but somehow, I had let a sense of disconnection seep in, subtly robbing me of a beautiful aspect of my identity.

The complexities of being a Black woman echoed louder than a firetruck speeding to extinguish a blazing fire. I found myself in unfamiliar rooms, feeling like an outsider simply because of my darker complexion. I was the passionate, outspoken Black woman whose voice rose as she expressed her concerns, yet I was unfairly labeled as angry or seen as overly aggressive. The question of where I truly belonged and the relevance of my skin tone gnawed at me. Did I enjoy more privileges and entitlements than my Black and brown sisters because of my lighter skin? Was I proud of my Black identity, or was I misunderstood as a Black woman? These were the questions that echoed within.

THE WORLD INSIDE AND OUT

*"We live in a world of constant juxtaposition
between joy that's possible and pain that's all
too common. We hope for love and success and
abundance, but we never quite forget that there is
always lurking the possibility of disaster"*
—*Marianne Williamson*

Imagine being a turtle, snugly ensconced within your protective shell, safe from the outside world. But one day, curiosity gets the best of you, and you venture to peek your head out. Once you do, there's no turning back. What you see and experience can't be erased. It lingers, imprinted in your memory. No matter how many times you retreat into your shell, you can't forget what you've seen and sensed.

I had spent my entire life within the only world I had ever known. It was comfortable, familiar, and secure. I meandered through life at my own pace, without the constraints of rules or expectations. Life had no instructions; it certainly didn't come with a manual. Inside my shell, I followed a routine that came naturally to me. But after years of this sheltered existence, my shell finally cracked, leaving me exposed and vulnerable to external forces. What had once been a protective fortress was now compromised.

Unexpectedly, I started seeing things I had never seen before and feeling pain in places I didn't know could hurt. My peaceful world, once quiet and serene, was now filled with unfamiliar sounds. I had been thrust into a new and bewildering reality. My once-impervious shell had been shattered, and I was left to navigate this unfamiliar terrain.

Once outside, I gazed at myself, trying to make sense of my reflection. It was the first time I had ever pondered the concept of self-identity. We shared similar size, color, and shape, but I struggled to define the likeness I saw. I had only known what existed inside my shell, and now, I had to adapt to a world I had never experienced before. No matter how many times I retreated to the comfort of my shell, it could never fully regain its original state. The world around me had left me questioning my place and the reasons behind my departure from the safe, protective confines of my shell.

We all desire, or perhaps wish, for a perfect world. But the world we live in is far from perfect, filled with people of diverse colors, sizes, shapes, backgrounds, and beliefs. I was once an innocent baby girl, oblivious to the harsh realities of this cruel and unforgiving world. However, I soon encountered the challenges and complexities of growing up as a Black child with a lighter complexion.

My formative years were spent in my grandmother's care, an environment untouched by discussions on skin tones or racial divisions. There were no pep talks about people looking or being different. Life was just life, and people were just people. I was a kid growing up under my grandmother's loving care, and it was all very ordinary.

But the day came when my grandmother left my world, not for a short errand, but forever. I never saw her again, and her absence shattered the world I knew. I found myself in unfamiliar territory, forced to face a world I had never known existed. It was a world where I was no longer just a girl but a "pretty light-skinned girl" with "long, thick hair." Words that had never been uttered inside my shell.

Questions arose. What did these labels mean, and

why were they significant? I was now being defined by my looks and skin tone, and that meant something. I wanted to understand what it meant and why it mattered.

Suddenly, I wasn't just a girl anymore; I was the "pretty light-skinned girl" with "long, thick hair." I had become defined by multiple external attributes. I yearned to explore this new aspect of my identity, to learn something about myself that I hadn't considered before. The real questions were: *How Black am I? Had I remained inside my shell for so long that I had lost touch with what truly mattered—my culture, my heritage, my history, my values, and, above all, my Black identity?*

LITTLE BLACK GIRL

"If you have the privilege of being born a Black woman, it is my belief that it is a part of your divine mission to liberate yourself from all external and internalized oppression and thereby liberate the world." —*Anna Yawson*

Life was once beautiful, simple and easy when looking at her. I looked at her in the mirror, and I saw a carefree girl. The girl I saw knew nothing of beauty standards or labels. She was simply a child, free of the constraints of judgment. The hue of her skin held no significance; it was just her skin. Her hair, whether curly or straight, long or short, was merely hair.

There was no need for self-discovery, no call for definition. She reveled in playful games and chatted with imaginary friends, laughing as she spun around in the world's embrace. Her authenticity shone brightly, illuminating the room. She didn't need to be anyone else; she was enough as herself, untouched by concerns about shade or appearance.

Her days were filled with the love and embrace of her cherished grandmother. Their connection went beyond words, transcending definition. She was precious, and everything around her held immeasurable value. Her world was one of safety and comfort, undisturbed by the concept of fear. She didn't have to escape her world or mend shattered dreams; she was free to be herself.

She lived in the moment, making simple plans for her tomorrows, like choosing which dress to wear. Although she sometimes wondered about her absent mother, her grandmother was the unshakable safety net. She knew she wasn't perfect, but the word "perfect" held no expectations for her.

However, life took an unexpected turn. Grief, a concept too complex for a child, entered her world as she grappled with the concept of loss. The person she knew as Grandma was gone, and her cherished world was transformed by death, confusion, and panic. She was left bewildered and dazed, uncertain of her identity without her grandmother. The world she once knew had shifted profoundly.

As a child, she couldn't comprehend what lay ahead. One thing was clear—her previously untouched, imperfect world had been exchanged for something unknown. She remembered the joy of wearing her pink dress, white tights, and patent leather shoes, celebrating unforgettable moments. Some lessons were straightforward, while others emerged as she navigated the defining moments of her life. There were things she could never have known until she experienced them firsthand.

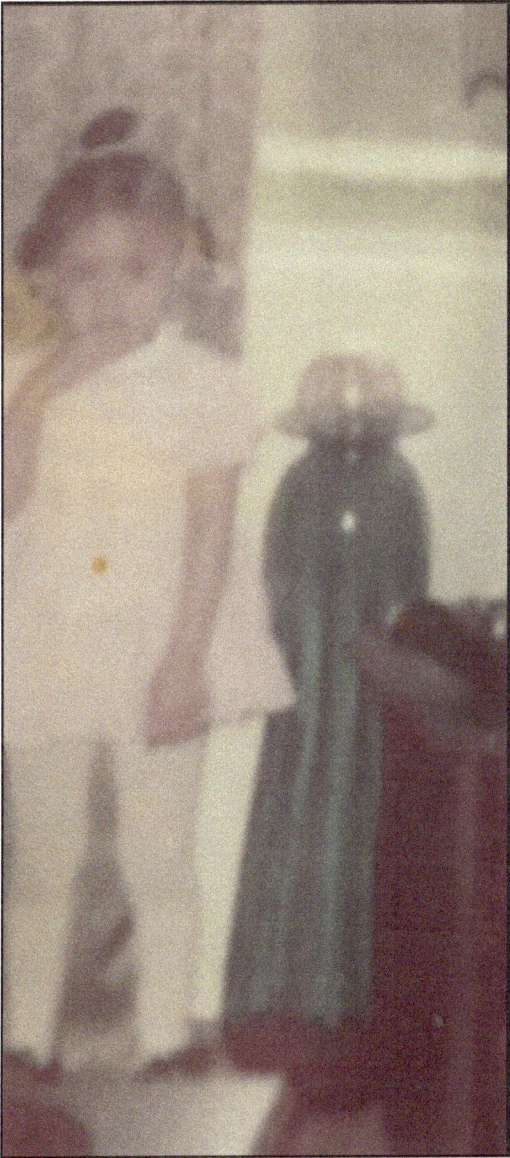

THE PLANTED SEED

"The tiny seed knew that in order to grow it needed to be dropped in dirt, covered in darkness, and struggle to reach the light." —Sandra Kring

I'm a Baltimore girl who grew up in the city. My grandmother was my caregiver until she passed away on February 8, 1978, just a month before my sixth birthday. Although my mother was present, she wasn't really there for me, so my grandmother took on all the responsibilities. When she died, we had to leave the only home I had ever known and move in with relatives I hardly knew.

I was about seven years old when my life took a dark turn for various reasons. Soon after we moved in with our relatives, a male family member started touching me in ways that were completely unfamiliar and inappropriate. I didn't understand what was happening or how to react. He would tell me how pretty I was, but did that excuse his actions? I couldn't make sense of it at the time. As time went on, his behavior escalated, and I began to believe that it was somehow related to my appearance. I started associating being pretty with giving him permission to touch me. These experiences, among many others, led me to believe that my looks were the only thing that mattered when it came to attracting men.

After we left that family, we moved in with my paternal aunt and uncle. They would often comment on how I was a pretty, light-skinned girl, emphasizing that I resembled my father's side of the family. My mother was more connected to that side of the family than I was. It made me wonder what was so significant about being a "pretty, light-skinned girl." *Pretty* and *light skinned* kept presenting itself, but it seemed like it carried some sort of meaning. Did looking like them only depend on having a lighter complexion? Were all light-skinned people supposed to look the same? Did your worth only come from being light-skinned? These were heavy thoughts for a young girl, but the importance placed on how I looked couldn't be ignored. It was clearly seen as a desirable attribute that needed to be acknowledged. Hearing these things from two different sets of family members didn't make it any clearer or easier to understand at the time.

Sometime in the late '80s, during my teenage years, I started to despise myself. Ironically, I used the very thing I despised, my appearance, to seek attention and gain acceptance among the "pretty, light-skinned girls' club." However, being pretty and having lighter skin came with a price. I didn't want to identify as Black because, in my mind, it was simply a matter of skin color and not a matter of race. Lightness was considered superior and came with undeniable privileges, which I started to enjoy.

I buried that violated little girl inside me and tried not to think about the traumas and pains of my childhood. I had retreated into a shell, isolated from a world where my worth was determined by my hair, pain, trauma, and skin tone. That little girl wished she had never been introduced to the harsh realities of the world, a world that began to define her solely based on superficial attributes.

I was no longer the innocent girl in the pink dress, black shoes, and pigtails. The girl who used to hide away in her shell, in the world her grandmother created, wished she had never been exposed to the unknown-the world before she was defined by her appearance, hair, suffering, trauma, and skin color. So, without knowing it was trauma at the time, I embraced that pain and allowed it to shape my life. Yes, I was a young Black girl who had been molested. He would tell me it was because I was pretty, as if that justified the harm he caused me. This twisted my understanding of beauty-being pretty had become ugly. I had no outlet for these emotions; they were trapped inside me, tightly sealed, requiring a miracle to release them.

The seed of pain had taken root and grown out of control. I became bitter and angry, with no guidance to help me understand or define my impulsive and reckless behavior, as I lived in the privileged world of being a light-skinned pretty girl that my paternal family valued the most. I found satisfaction in provoking resentment among darker-skinned girls, flaunting my good looks, long hair, and lighter skin in their faces simply because I could. In high school and in my neighborhood, I was oblivious to how my actions made darker young girls feel, only fueling their dislike for me. I brushed it off as jealousy, ignorant to the fact that my behavior disgusted them. I thought, *Don't hate on me because I'm light-skinned*, without considering how my words and actions were impacting them in such a negative way.

It was easy for me to say, "You're black and ugly."

To me, darkness was not attractive. Unfortunately, this mindset of "lighter is better" had been ingrained in me by my family. As a result, black girls questioned why they were so dark, struggling to embrace and accept the beauty of their own black skin. The darker young black girls didn't realize that my conflicting thoughts had everything to do with me and nothing to do with them.

My own insecurities made me feel better by making them feel worse. I used my light skin as a shield to hide my own deep-rooted self-doubt. It went beyond simply being a young black light-skinned girl; I wasn't addressing the real issue at all. I had created a false sense of superiority and an unapologetic attitude that said, "Deal with it." I found a sense of security under the divide between dark and light skin tones, which allowed me to stir up more animosity among darker girls.

I weakened my darker-skinned sisters emotionally, from the crown of their heads to the soles of their feet, driving them further into hatred for me. I had lost control as a child, and the one thing I could control was capitalizing on my skin tone. So, I took advantage of it and continued to revel in my privilege.

When I was around 16 years old, my cousin and I used to call ourselves "Salt and Pepper". One evening, while walking down the street, we encountered two young boys who approached us wanting to talk and get to know us. One of the boys immediately said, "I want the light-skinned, pretty one."

It wasn't clear how my cousin felt about that comment, but she smiled and responded, "But I have the body, though." She had a shapely figure, which was a trait common among the women on my dad's side of the family. However, I still felt superior to her because being light-skinned was more socially desirable than having a curvy physique.

My father's side of the family had a preference for lighter-skinned individuals and treated them better, including myself. While looking beyond the surface, my cousin, who had brown skin, once again had to navigate through a mix of emotions related to colorism, by trying to downplay her hurt feelings and highlighting her physical attributes. She was always in competition for attention, growing up with four light-skinned sisters, one considered light brown, and a light-skinned mother with long, straight hair.

My cousin resembled her father in looks and complexion, and was often referred to as "the darker one." Looking back, I should have stood up against the hurt caused by those boys, but I remained silent, giving power to the words, "I want the light-skinned, pretty one"-the same power I granted to the family member who molested me.

My cousin often expressed feeling like the outsider in the family because of her darker skin. Despite that, I was too caught up in the compliments and my own light-skinned privilege, as my cousin gave me a smug look that seemed to say, "I told you so." I suppose she wanted me to feel like she possessed something I didn't-a beautiful and curvy body. But it didn't bother me because in my world, light and bright was always considered superior to dark-skinned individuals. As a young teenage girl, I was unbelievably naive and self-centered, unaware of the harm I was causing. Little did I know that my actions, thoughts, and beliefs were part of a larger issue, which specifically affects darker-skinned women. At the time, I had no idea that my behaviors had a name—Colorism.

HATE AT FIRST SIGHT

Love at first sight > attraction
Hate at first sight > intriguing
Love at person's good deeds > respect
Hate at person's good deeds > insecurity
Love as days pass by > friendship
Hate as days pass by > addicted
— Woofaslan

In January 1990, just two months away from my 18th birthday, I found myself working as a part-time student at Johns Hopkins Hospital. One day, as I glanced up from my desk, there she stood, striding into the office with an air of confidence that could make you think she owned the place – or at least, that's how it appeared to me. In that very moment, my initial thought was, *She must think she's all that...* or maybe, *Does she believe she's all that?* She had a light complexion, a tall stature, exuded beauty, was impeccably dressed, possessed long flowing hair, and her walk carried a hint of sassiness.

I didn't know this woman at all, yet I was quick to judge. Little did I understand then what I realize now. I projected my own internal biases and prejudices, rooted in the color of our skin, onto other light-skinned females. I found myself doing to her what had been done to me by darker-skinned women – that's "hating at first sight."

I was light-skinned and pretty, sporting long hair, just like her; what set her apart from me? Why did I cast such a scrutinizing gaze her way when she was essentially a mirror image of myself – light-skinned? I found myself wondering, "Is she a shade lighter, and did that somehow make her more beautiful in my eyes?" It left me feeling somewhat intimidated. Was she competition? Her fancy attire and footwear, was I envious of them? Was I possibly jealous? Well, it's hard to say for sure. Was my aversion to her driven by a sense of threat? I couldn't quite fathom the myriad questions racing through my mind and why, all of a sudden, being light-skinned no longer seemed as significant. Why had I allowed her to diminish my sense of worth and attractiveness? Were these the same emotions experienced by women with darker complexions? I was left in a situation that made me feel as though I shared the same feelings of inadequacy as darker-skinned Black women.

History seemed to be replaying itself, and I remained oblivious to its underlying pain. The full extent and true meaning of colorism continued to elude me, as I had never encountered that word during my upbringing within my protective shell. Nevertheless, I was fully immersed in discriminatory behaviors without even realizing it.

It's a well-documented fact that during the era of slavery, lighter-skinned slaves were often assigned domestic duties, while their darker-skinned counterparts were compelled to toil in the harsh conditions of the fields. Lighter-skinned slaves were considered more privileged, a distinction that understandably sowed seeds of tension and animosity among their darker-skinned fellow slaves. Yet, I grappled with the question of how I could justify the sentiments I had towards my light-skinned counterpart, considering we shared the exact same skin tone.

The paper bag test was a discriminatory practice utilized in the hiring of Black individuals: "If someone's skin color matched or was lighter than a paper bag, they would gain entry or be considered for employment. Anyone darker than the paper bag's shade would be excluded." This approach, rooted in evaluating skin color, has historically fueled judgments and decision-making processes, perpetuating a socially divisive system founded on skin color.

As I reflect on that day when I watched her approach me with a sense of disdain, it's clear that there was no valid explanation for the intense and misplaced emotions I harbored merely due to the tone of her skin. Deep down, I realized the need to amend the negativity that had taken root in my mind. After all, she had no more control over her skin tone than darker-skinned women had over their shade. It was essential for me to change how I perceived her, and I did.

As soon as she greeted me with a warm smile and extended her hand while saying, "Welcome," my prior judgments about her being lighter no longer held any validity. I was determined not to remain entangled in a system or mindset that elevated lightness over darkness or perpetuated the notion of light-skinned privilege dividing "Us" from "Them." Neither of us owed anyone an explanation for being born Black, beautiful, and light-skinned; we simply were. In a world that relentlessly attempts to sow division based on the color of our skin, we must resist and promote unity, rejecting the empowerment of hate.

Let's return to celebrating our shared identity as Black and proud women rather than conforming to the standards of light versus dark. By the way, Miss K and I eventually became the best of friends, and our bond had nothing to do with our skin tone; it was all about our character. We mustn't ignore, turn a blind eye to, or be deaf to what's right in front of us: the insidious presence of colorism, which is a pervasive footprint of racism.

USE WHAT YOU GOT
TO GET WHAT YOU WANT

"The first step to getting what you want is to have the courage to get rid of what you don't." —Zig Ziglar

In my mid-20s, a mother of three sons, and having gone through the turbulence of toxic relationships and divorce, I grappled with embracing my identity as a proud Black woman. But as life unfolded, I couldn't help but notice how frequently I was told how pretty and light-skinned I was. It became apparent that lighter skin was perceived as more attractive and garnered extra attention. I decided to take advantage of it. It was undeniable that I received preferential treatment and could often get my way just because of my complexion. I'd often hear remarks like, "You're lucky you're so pretty with that light-skinned glow," and I would occasionally throw temper tantrums, knowing that my light-skinned privileges could work in my favor.

I flaunted my looks with a swipe of red lipstick that complemented my fair skin, making my lips seem fuller and my complexion even brighter. I perpetuated the belief that I was superior and more attractive than darker-skinned women, which allowed me to assert my presence in any room, regardless of their fashion sense or physical attributes. Even if they dressed impeccably or had more voluptuous curves, I considered my light skin an unbeatable asset.

By this point, I understood what I was doing, even though I was unaware of the term "colorism." I recognized that my actions were pushing women with darker skin tones further into feelings of insecurity and self-doubt about their complexion. Had I known the origins, definitions, and implications of colorism, could it have made a difference in my behavior, even though I was perpetuating the same pain that this system had created?

I was never raised or taught to be this way, but as I grew older, societal pressures ensnared me like a suffocating serpent. I found myself trapped in a world that categorized people based on their skin tone and determined how they should be treated. I became a light-skinned Black woman who used her looks to her advantage and bullied others in the process. I remained stuck in this cycle for years, viewing it as a tool for self-gain without any excuses. Unbeknownst to me, this mindset severely affected my self-esteem, self-love, and self-worth. If I didn't receive the attention I felt entitled to, I'd automatically assume something was wrong with me. I believed my lighter skin, along with my physical appearance, was the sole definition of who I was. I disregarded any other aspects of myself. I manipulated my thoughts into believing that I was doing nothing wrong and inadvertently became complicit in a system I didn't even realize was an issue until recent years. I perpetuated deep-seated racism, categorizing women based on their skin tone, contributing to the notion that lighter skin was more desirable than darker skin. I enjoyed responding to labels like "Hey, red!" or "Hey, yellow!" because they played into the privilege I held due to my lighter complexion.

Throughout my life, I used my skin color to mask the internal pain I was experiencing. I continued to revolve in this cycle, attempting to validate my light-skinned privilege. I projected an outward image of confidence and self-assuredness, but deep down, I struggled to feel validated. I was merely using what society had conditioned me to believe was important. The complex issues surrounding colorism may not have a quick solution, but the fight to address them must continue. We must stand together, united as both dark-and light-skinned Black women, rather than apart.

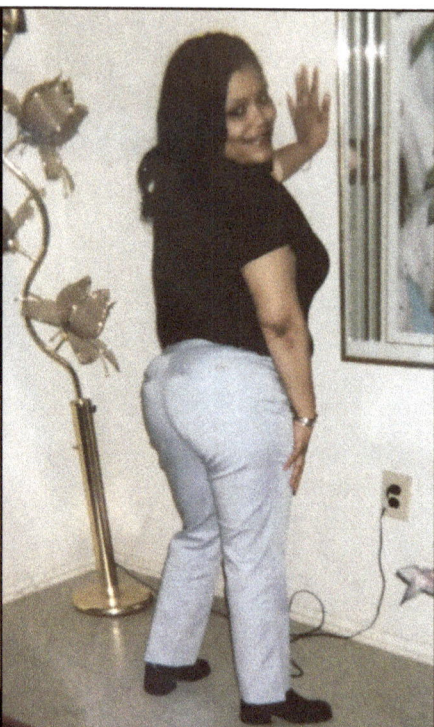

SHIFTING THE ATMOSPHERE

"Make every effort to change things you do not like. If you cannot make a change, change the way you have been thinking. You might find a new solution."
— Maya Angelou

Now, in my fifties as a Black woman, I've traversed a myriad of experiences that have had a cultural and personal impact not only on me but on countless Black and brown women worldwide. As an educated woman of color, fully aware of the advantages that come with being a light-skinned Black woman, it's evident that colorism remains a glaring issue. While it attempts to radiate as brightly as the sun against the deep blue sky, I can't ignore its debilitating and divisive influence. If I continue to hide in the shadows of colorism, pretending that skin tones no longer hold sway in our present-day lives, then colorism prevails, perpetuating an overwhelmingly negative impact on our darker and brown-skinned sisters. The choice was clear: either I change, evolve, and grow beyond the conflicting notions of my light-skinned privilege or remain entangled in the web of discriminatory colorism and shadeism. I could no longer remain ignorant, blind, or deaf to the stark realities of colorism.

Once upon a time, I was blissfully unaware of the existence and origins of colorism, racism, prejudices, and biases. However, I came face to face with the "light-skinned pretty girl syndrome," a reality I could no longer ignore. My past experiences could no longer hold me hostage, forcing me to rely on my lighter skin to get ahead in life and relationships. This phenomenon, deeply rooted in society, has persisted for generations, causing division, isolation, segregation, discrimination, and disadvantages against darker-skinned women.

As Black women of any shade, we must all become more conscious of the ways in which our actions and choices can inadvertently hurt and retraumatize one another based on the color, tone, or shade of our skin. In many respects, I had felt like I lived in a different world compared to my Black and brown sisters. I had distanced myself from the mirror image of beauty and strength that society often overlooked in Black women with darker skin. We shared the same Black identity, with various shades of skin tones, yet I perceived myself as somehow superior, different, and more beautiful. I knew I had to change the narrative not just for myself, but for all my sisters.

I choose to be Black and beautiful; Black and bold; Black and brilliant; Black and educated; Black and inclusive; Black and powerful; Black and professional; Black and proud; Black and relentless; Black and unashamed. My Black identity transcends the shade of my skin tone. Women of color have been silenced in shame for far too long, deprived of a voice to speak, to fight, and to advocate. Women of color have faced challenges beyond colorism, just as women's right to vote, pay inequality, and gender inequality were once pressing issues. Nevertheless, the influence of skin tone remains a pervasive factor across many parts of the world, causing us to relive history instead of making it.

We must never forget the sacrifices and unwavering commitment of countless Black women who have transformed history, leaving their legacies as blueprints for continued progress. Prominent Black women such as Maya Angelou, Coretta Scott King, Harriet Tubman, Rosa Parks, and many others have dedicated themselves to combating racial inequalities, colorism, racism, biases, and prejudices while advocating for women's rights. The first Black woman elected to Congress, Shirley A. Chisholm, in 1968, Michelle Obama as the first Black woman in the White House in 2008, Kamala Harris as the first Black and only woman Vice President in 2020, and Ketanji Brown Jackson's historic appointment to the U.S. Supreme Court in 2022 demonstrate our progress in overcoming underrepresentation. Let's not turn against each other because of our melanin levels, whether we are darker than brown or lighter than caramel. Though our skin colors may vary, we should not allow them to divide us.

As the lyrics in "Fabulous" featuring Ne-Yo suggest, "I'm a movement by myself, but I'm a force when we're together." Let's seize the power of Black women together, be the force for the change we all desire, and uplift one another. Let's dismantle colorism and enhance the futures of dark-and light-skinned women by breaking down barriers and uniting as empowered women of color at the same table.

"Though some argue that colorism can affect people of all skin tones, people who are darker-skinned are known to bear the brunt of it." —Alycea Gayle

I APOLOGIZE.

I'm sorry for my ignorance!
I'm sorry that I hurt you!
I'm sorry I caused you pain!
I'm sorry I projected a form of racism onto your life!
I'm sorry I made you feel uncomfortable in your beautiful
black and brown skin!
I'm sorry I created two separate worlds between us!
I'm sorry I was unapologetic towards your feelings!
I'm sorry that I was an uneducated Black woman to the
systemic hate of Colorism... I apologize! Please forgive me!

JUANIKA BALLARD, 44

Juanika Ballard, a native of Baltimore, Maryland. She is passionate about educating, encouraging, and supporting our youth.

Over the course of several decades, Ballard has dedicated herself to giving back to her community in diverse and impactful ways. Her unwavering commitment to cultivating and uplifting youth has been a driving force in her life. Her experiences included teaching fourth-grade summer school, coaching basketball in Baltimore City Public

Schools' and serving as a counselor in a program sponsored by Johns Hopkins School of Mental Health, designed to support children with emotional and mental disorders.

Today, Juanika remains passionate about mentoring youth and young adults, as well as coaching youth basketball. Her belief in being the catalyst for positive change in her community is the guiding principle by which she lives. She purposefully strives to make a profound impact on the lives of the youth she encounters.

With a career spanning over two decades, Juanika is a seasoned law enforcement officer. Her diverse experiences have taken her through various precincts and specialized units, but it was her role as a school resource officer that she held as her most meaningful contribution.

Education has always been a priority for Juanika. She holds a bachelor's degree in applied psychology from Coppin State University and a master's degree in pastoral counseling from Loyola University Maryland. Committed to ongoing learning, she actively seeks out additional training and seminars across various fields of interest.

In her entrepreneurial capacity, Juanika serves as the CEO and founder of Eagles and Owls Consulting, LLC. The company specializes in providing personal safety training to employees who offer in-home services.

Juanika, along with her spouse, has celebrated nearly 15 years of marriage and is blessed with five wonderful children and two cherished grandchildren.

Juanika Ballard exemplifies dedication, leadership, and a passion for community service, making her a valuable contributor in various aspects of life, from law enforcement to education and mentorship.

ACKNOWLEDGMENT

A special thank you to my parents, grandparents, aunts and children. The sum total of me is made up of the best parts of you all. I also want to acknowledge my mentors and the exceptional people who have planted and watered seeds in all stages of my life, helping me to grow into the person I am today. Your gifts and sacrifices will positively impact generations to come.

DEDICATION

I dedicate this writing to my spouse, Monica Williams. You have always believed in me and encouraged me to be the greatest version of myself, and you have supported me as I evolved physically, mentally, emotionally and spiritually. Thank you!

COLORISM DEFINED

"Colorism is a symptom and system of oppression."
—Sarah L. Webb

Colorism is the practice of discrimination in which those with lighter skin are treated more favorably than those with darker skin. Colorism often happens within the same race. It is believed that this practice is the product of racism in the United States and upholds the white standard of beauty in the institution of oppression. Racism is defined as the individual, cultural and institutional beliefs and discrimination that systematically oppress people of color. Discrimination is the mistreatment of an individual or group based on their social membership, regardless of their social power.

The term "colorism" is believed to have been coined by novelist Alice Walker in 1982. It refers not only to the preference for lighter skin between different racial and ethnic communities but also within those communities. Colorism is an enduring vestige of colonialism and white dominance around the globe and disproportionately harms women of color.

COLORISM'S VENOM

"Forgiveness means that you fill yourself with love and you radiate that love outward and refuse to hang onto the venom or hatred that was engendered by the behaviors that caused the wounds." —Wayne Dye

Colorism has inflicted deep wounds on families and communities throughout generations. It is believed that during the era of slavery, the offspring of slave masters and slaves, who happened to have lighter skin, often received more favorable treatment and privileges. This preference was not solely based on the child's parentage but also on the perception that lighter-skinned individuals possessed distinct advantages.

It is also believed that slave masters exhibited a preference for darker-skinned women due to their pronounced features and curves, which were deemed attractive. Regrettably, less attention has been given to the experiences of lighter-skinned slaves who were subjected to the same heinous acts by their masters.

Slave owners frequently engaged in the sexual exploitation of their slaves, resulting in the birth of light-skinned children. These individuals were afforded preferential treatment, often assigned domestic tasks, while their darker-skinned counterparts toiled in the fields, performing more physically demanding labor. This favoritism toward lighter-skinned slaves was not only a consequence of their parentage but was also rooted in the unfounded beliefs that they were superior in intelligence and beauty.

The "paper bag test" found frequent use within Black communities and during the hiring of Black individuals in the 19th and 20th centuries. It entailed a simple criterion: those whose skin matched or was lighter than a paper bag were granted access to certain spaces or considered for employment, while those with darker skin were denied such opportunities.

Colorism manifests differently across cultures and time periods, but a recurring theme often links negative connotations to darker skin tones while attaching positive attributes to lighter complexions.

In specific Asian societies, a strong preference for fair, pale skin persists. This preference arises from the belief that individuals with lighter skin could afford to avoid outdoor labor and remain indoors, symbolizing higher social status. Historically, Europe shared a similar perspective, with those possessing "blue veins" or "blue blood" (referring to pale skin that made veins appear bluish) being considered of "noble" and "unblemished" lineage. However, contemporary Western society has seen a surge in the popularity of tanned skin among Caucasians, signifying luxury associated with leisure and vacations.

Reflecting on history, it is impossible not to empathize with the individuals affected by colorism. It has perpetuated a painful and toxic reality for Black women, particularly concerning the diverse range of skin tones. Many untold stories of discrimination, racism, and colorism persist, leaving one to imagine the profound impact of the divisions based on skin tone, especially between darker-skinned and lighter-skinned women. This segregation rooted in skin tones has led me to question my place in the ongoing narrative of colorism, a narrative that continues to inflict psychological, emotional, and sometimes physical harm, further straining relationships among women of color.

As a Black woman with a lighter brown complexion,

often described as "caramel," I find myself straddling both sides of this divide. I am undoubtedly Black, yet I ponder whether my lighter skin may have influenced distinct treatment and provided certain advantages, akin to those with even lighter tones. Skin tones have shaped the experiences of women of color in multifaceted ways, and the legacy of colorism remains an ever-present facet of our lives.

A CHILD'S PERSPECTIVE

"We must not allow other people's limited perceptions to define us." —Virginia Satir

As we explore my journey and experience of colorism, I am reminded that perspective also plays a part in how one navigates through life. At a very young age, I learned that listening to your elders was very important. If an elder told you to do something, you did it without question. It did not matter if you liked or disliked that task; it had to be followed. With that idea in mind, I often found myself listening to elders as they spoke amongst themselves. It seemed to take me a little while to realize that listening to elders as they spoke amongst themselves was not a part of that idea. After years of processing, I must conclude that if one chooses to listen to elders as they speak amongst themselves, know that they may or may not be trying to "one up" the other.

I vaguely recall visiting family one evening, and my maternal grandmother's sister was present. My aunt was admired, well respected and loved by everyone. However, like most families, there always seemed to be a hint of shade and pettiness whenever she came around. My grandmother and her sisters were all light-skinned. Growing up, I thought they were white. I am told that my great-grandmother was Black and Native American. My grandmother's father was Black and Irish, making her very light-skinned.

When my aunt came around, everyone seemed to turn up the phony until she left. She was always "put together." She, unlike my grandmother, wore make up and designer clothing. My aunt was a Mary Kay consultant and was always looking for an opportunity to show off her merchandise by wearing it. Her skin was always even and shiny from multiple applications of foundation, neatly drawn-on eyebrows and bright red lipstick-covered lips. Her bleached blonde hair pulled back into a tight bun, she was always wearing gawky jewelry, large jeweled rings, necklaces, earrings and newly purchased or dry-cleaned sparkly outfits. This is where the philosophies clash. Always listen to your elder's but stay out of grown folks' business. Obviously, without anywhere to go, and with no internet or cell phones to occupy my time, I sat and waited while the elders talked, careful not to let them know I was listening and all in "their" business. I learned to color with such focus and intensity as to not miss any of the juicy family tea. My aunt was known for bragging about her grandchildren. She had a way of making ordinary things seem exceptional. "My granddaughter washed her hands! My grandson tied his shoes."

All the while, they were eight and 16.

My cousins and I were coached not to tell her any of our family or household business because she would tell the world. At some point during the gathering, she learned that my mother and I were moving from Baltimore City to Baltimore County. In the early 80's and 90's, Baltimore County, specifically Owing Mills, was known to be predominately white, with very few minorities of any race. I sat and listened while my aunt shared stories of unprovoked attacks on Blacks by whites. I cannot say for certain that she had accurate and confirmed accounts of Blacks being assaulted or kidnapped by whites in Baltimore County, but I knew everything she said invoked fear. I distinctly remember her looking me square in my eyes with the deepest look of sincerity and alarm; she told me to be careful around white people, as any perceived wrong doing or dismay could lead to me mysteriously disappearing and later being discovered hanged. Lynched?! Was she serious?

My kindergarten teacher was white, and I never thought the idea of hanging Black people, nevertheless a kid, crossed her mind.

Upon reflection, I find the mere thought of such an act traumatic—imagine processing that as a nine-year-old child who was excited about moving to a larger, safer home, which so happened to be where there were more white people than I had ever seen in my entire life. Her "words of caution" played through my mind as we packed, drove and moved into the new townhouse. Now, with so much negativity in my mind from the words of my aunt, the excitement of moving turned into suspicion and anxiety. This was beyond dark-skinned versus light-skinned, privilege versus mistreatment because of the tone of one's skin. I was concerned about staying alive and hoping I did not lose my life at the hands of a white person because I was Black. Regardless of my skin tone, this was more alarming.

Shortly after moving in, my cousin asked me to meet her at the basketball court. She provided me with clear details so I would not miss the hidden cut-through to the elementary school courts. Getting there was easy. I followed her directions exactly and found the basketball court with no problem. The challenge was finding my way home. I was so focused on looking for the cut-through that I failed to pay attention to my surroundings leading to the cut-through. Not long after leaving the basketball court, I found myself at an unfamiliar intersection. Heading to the basketball court, I never noticed that I had biked on an overpass over a stream. I recall approaching the intersection and instantly being stricken with fear. Several people were out doing yard work, but they were all white. I did not know what to do next. I was afraid to bike further for fear that I was going the wrong way and would never make it home. I was also deathly afraid to approach the white people tending to their lawns. I froze and began to cry hysterically. After some time, a white lady approached and offered me assistance. I was reluctant to tell her that I was lost. I did not want to tell her where I lived because then, she'd know where to drag me away from after dark.

With great reservation, I told her where I lived, only for her to say, "Which Timbergrove Road?"

Oh no. Wait, there's more than one? Where was I exactly? After verifying the different locations, she gave me directions to my house. Silly me; I was literally down the street from my house. I had never been so happy to be home. That night, I did not sleep much, preparing to fight back if she did show up to lynch me. From that point on, numerous white people have made a mockery of my aunt's warning and advice. Days, weeks and months soon had turned into years, and yet, I was still alive with not one lynching experience. Although this theory sounded crazy, as a little girl, I was left to believe the words that came out of the mouth of my elder. As unpleasant as it was to live in panic over being hanged, the complexities of colorism held hands with racism, and that could not be ignored. If only we could see past light and dark, black and white and the ramifications that cause separation between women, people and a generation as a whole. How much better could the world be if we, as a society, stop clashing with our privileges and work with our similarities instead? Maybe light-skinned Black people were not accurate sources of information about white people. I wondered what was ahead of me and how much of it would surround my academics or my skin tone. Nonetheless, I was certain about leaving behind the perceptions of fears my aunt instilled in me concerning people who did not look like me. The fall of 1989 was the start of many years attending school as a minority, and I was certain there was more to learn about the culture surrounding me.

COLOR CRAZED

"You cannot change what you are, only what you do."
—Philip Pullman

As a child, I spent the summer with my paternal grandparents. My grandfather worked most of the time, so interaction with him was seldom. I am sure working as a produce selector in the 1950s lended itself to several racially tense encounters. My grandfather never uttered a single negative word about his experience around us. I never witnessed him frustrated or upset after a long day's work. My grandmother, a Sioux Indian from Chief Sitting Bull's tribe, was a huge influence in shaping my perspective and understanding of the world and my role within it. My grandparents had 10 children, four sons and six daughters, all of whom are various shades of brown beauty.

No one on my father's side of the family was extremely light or dark, which may explain why colorism was never welcomed in our home. I recall my cousin rambling on about how she was better because she was light-skinned, and her darker-skinned brother was less-than. If it were in her nature to verbally scold us, she would have told my cousin how ridiculous she sounded. In the sweetest, yet sternest way, my grandmother attempted to redirect my cousin's thinking by saying, "It takes all kinds of people to make the world go around."

The idea that one is better or worse than another merely because of skin tone was what my grandmother referred to as "Color Crazed." Believing that some were better, safer or smarter merely due to the color of their skin was absurd. The conversation shifted after someone expressed a commonly shared philosophy that Blacks should dislike Whites. I was not sure how to feel about my cousin assuming she was better than me because she was light—yes, I took it personally. It was important for me to understand the rationale behind her thinking and when she learned to think like that. As stated, those conversations were never held within my paternal grandmother's home. Besides the lynching stories my maternal aunt told, I was not placed in a skin tone or "black and white" category within my family. I must admit, it was a sensitive topic, and I wondered if I had to now be compared to girls my age with lighter skin, something that was not an issue before then. We went from playing outside, being children, with no cares in the world to worrying about light, dark, white and being lynched.

My grandmother grew up in the 1930s after The Great Depression. She was not an outlier on the shades of brown spectrum, not very light or dark. I am certain that she had colorism experiences and met several racist individuals in her lifetime. However, those interactions did not develop into stereotypes across shades, races or nationalities.

My grandmother quickly stated, "What has a white person ever done to you?"

Of course, my answer was, "Nothing."

She had a way with words. She did not yell much or degrade us, but I could see the disappointment in her eyes. My grandmother told me it was more important to judge a person based on how they treated me, not by the color of their skin. I can hear the words of the great and infamous Martin Luther King Jr.: "I have a dream that my four little children will one day live in a nation where they will not be judged by the color of their skin but by the content of their character."

If a person has not wronged you in any way, negative thoughts or beliefs about them are simply wrong and unfair. It was during this time that I learned empathy. What if someone looked at you and thought you were mean or bad simply because you are tall? How would you feel? That perspective sticks with me today. I spent so much time at the feet of my grandmother, holding on to every word that came out of her mouth, wisdom coming from the east, west, north and south of her brain as she quietly spoke. When you walked away from her presence, you left feeling like a student in a classroom with the teacher looking over her eyeglasses, saying, "Today's lesson will be on..."

FEAR VS. RESPECT

*"Great changes may not happen right away, but with
effort even the difficult may become easy"*
—Bill Blackman

My father grew up in the 1960 s, during the civil rights movement. For him, the perspective on life and the "proper" place for a Black man was jaded and tainted. In the late 1970s, he joined the Marine Corps. He traveled to California for basic training. During that time, he experienced what must have been some of the most challenging times of his life—so challenging that he ultimately left sooner than intended. From that brief experience, he developed a strong level of distrust for white people. Not wanting me to be unprepared for adult life, he would often come to my grandparents' house late at night or early in the morning, full of conversation. He did not want "the white man" to tell me or make me feel like I did not matter. He shared countless African proverbs that highlighted the legacy of our intelligence and richness. I can hear him in my mind, saying, "You can do anything you want to as long as you put your mind to it."

The crazy thing about that is I really believed that there was nothing I could not do. I was too young, or maybe ignorant, to try and figure out if his discharge from the military had anything to do with racism. I cannot imagine it being due to his skin tone. Was that even a thing for males? I mean, my father was a medium brown shade, tall, thin, Black man. All things considered, he was home and did not converse with me about why he had returned. I did not know it then, but these lessons of positive self-worth and Black excellence would turn out to be very helpful later in life. Nonetheless, between my grandmother and father, I had just enough knowledge and understanding to prepare me for grade school.

In the middle of my fifth-grade school year, I moved from Baltimore City to Baltimore County. Initially, I was told that although I was academically advanced in Baltimore City Public Schools, I was behind in Baltimore County Public Schools. I knew I did not want to be known as the big Black dumb girl, but I did not have a clue of how to regain the status of "the smart girl" at school. As a result of that devastating news, I opted to explore bully characteristics. Let me just preface by saying I never physically assaulted anyone, but I will admit to posturing and speaking in a certain manner to intimidate others. I have always been above average height. I was so tall, kids thought it funny to call me "the Jolly Black Giant," an attempted play off of the infamous produce mascot, the Jolly Green Giant. Gaining respect and recognition was extremely important to me. I believed if I was respected, I would not need to fear being lynched or mistreated by others.

I recall telling someone, "You'd better be scared of me. I'm big. I'm Black. And I'm from Baltimore City. I'll beat you up."

That person responded, "But there's nothing scary about you, so why would I be scared?"

Truth be told, I was not an actual fighter. Prior to that, I had only orchestrated one-on-one fights with cousins and in the neighborhood. I needed to find and define myself. Over the summer, I spent time with my grandmother, learning priceless lessons about life, civility, love and family. My father and I often had deep intellectual conversations about life, purpose and the universe. With each conversation, he always left me something to ponder on until the next.

"It's better to be respected than feared."

If a person respects you, they will think of, interact with and treat you in a respectable manner at all times. However, if a person fears you, they are constantly thinking of ways to get back at you. A person who fears you will kill you. A person who respects you will reject ill thoughts and actions as they pertain to you. From that conversation, I knew the life of a bully was not the life for me, just as Black versus white or light-skinned versus dark-skinned were topics of conversation I had no desire to engage in nor were philosophies I wished to practice.

MEANINGFUL RELATIONSHIPS

*"Ever tried. Ever failed. No matter. Try Again. Fail
again. Fail better." —Samuel Beckett*

Throughout grade school, I developed friendships with
people from various cultural backgrounds. In Baltimore
City schools, I had plenty of Black friends. At this moment,
I cannot remember if the friend group was divided by skin
tone; my guess is that it was not. As kids, if you were outside,
we just played together. However, entering the Baltimore
County Public school system, the world was my oyster. As a
result of the small number of Black girls in attendance, we
had a choice. We could all get together and be friends and
exclude non-Blacks, or we could create friend groups with
people who were friendly to us. I chose to be friends with
friendly people.

I would be lying if I said there was not separation
amongst Black girls. The darker-skinned Black girls sat at a
table in the corner of the school cafeteria. This group was
almost impossible to enter. One would need to be obsessed
with boys, fashion and hair, being careful never to come
to school with a hair out of place or an outfit that was not
color-coordinated. Let me not forget the shoes: Sneakers
had to be crispy clean and white. None of those things were
important to me. I was solely focused on academic excellence
and athletics—no need to get your hair done weekly, only to
sweat it out on the basketball court the very next day. There
was also the light-skinned girls. They seemed to have the

hardest time joining a friend group. They were either too dark to be with the white girls or too light to be with the dark-skinned girls. These were challenges that kept my head spinning and had me wondering where I fit into all of this foolishness.

Navigating middle school with a lack of academic confidence was a disaster in the making. I recall trekking along, believing that I was average. I did not put much effort into academics, but I remained behaved. It was unacceptable to have the teacher call home to report negative behavior. I really struggled with mathematics. I just could not understand the concept. My math teacher offered after-school assistance, but I was unable to attend because I would have no way home from school if I did not ride the bus. I lived approximately three miles from the middle school. Although we had settled into our neighborhood well, I would not be granted permission to walk home alone from school.

Finally, one day, he placed his hand on my shoulder and sympathetically stated, "Maybe you're just one of those people who just doesn't get math."

And with that escape, I stopped trying because, surely, I was one of those people who just did not get math. I completed the school year with that average mindset. That year, I earned average markings—C's across the board. Although I was not happy with the grades, I began to accept the reality of my limitations. As much as I wanted to escape the ideals of racism, what actually did he mean by, "Maybe you're just one of those people who just doesn't get math"? What people were he referring to?

I remember receiving the seventh-grade schedule in the mail. It was in that mailer I learned where and what time my bus arrived, my home room section and teacher, and teachers for various academic classes and specials. I looked at the schedule and did not recognize one name in particular. Who was this mysterious math teacher? Was it a male or female, old or young, nice or mean? Never did I question whether the teacher was white or Black because I assumed the person would be white. After all, they all were. On the first day of school, I watched a Black lady pass through the halls. Immediately, I was intrigued. *Who's the Black lady? Is she a new teacher, office staff or cafeteria worker?* I soon found out she was, in fact, the person who would change my mathematical perception—in my sole, yet expert opinion, the best math teacher in the history of Baltimore County Public Schools. She was different—the epitome of Black excellence. She maintained a straight-faced and stern demeanor. She demanded respect and expected excellence. Initially, I was not fond of her classroom boundaries and teaching style. After receiving paperwork with constant corrections, she requested to speak with me after class. It was during that time I laid out my valid explanation for constant incorrect equations.

With confidence, I stated, "I'm just one of those people who is not good at math."

She looked at me with the most puzzled look upon her face. "What do you mean, you're 'just one of those people who just won't get math'? There's no such thing."

She offered lunch and after-school sessions to help me. I was initially reluctant to go for help during lunch because I was worried about what others thought. *Only dumb people go for remedial*, I thought. Truthfully, no one knew your grades unless you shared them. Others merely guessed based on the one-in-22 chance you were called upon and gave the wrong answer during class. For several days, she would say, "You didn't come to see me for lunch bunch," as she passed me in the halls. I would give some dumb, scripted excuse, but the truth was, I did not want others to know I did not understand what was being taught. I wasn't sure if I did not want people knowing I was struggling or if I did not want my white classmates to know. Finally, after failing a quiz,

I took her up on her offer. With my mother's permission meeting with my teacher became a regular routine until it was no longer necessary. The one-on-one tutoring helped tremendously and as a result my math grades improved. My maternal grandfather was so impressed with my academic performance that he promised me $10 for every A I received for each marking period. It was like God Himself opened the floodgates to heaven. Seventy dollars in the 1990's was like $1 million. It was then that I learned teachers are more inclined to help you if they see you're really trying. Most teachers want you to succeed.

After I shared my grandfather's promise with my teachers, they held me accountable when I was not in the mood for learning. Luckily for me, I had the same math teacher in eighth grade. She became not just my teacher, but my mentor. She reminded me of women in my family who demanded respect. My grandmother commanded a room upon entering it. She did not tolerate nonsense, and misbehaving—especially in public—was forbidden. My teacher was an at-school reminder of home and family expectations. In the classroom, she did not smile much, but when she did, it lit up and relaxed the room. She had a heart as soft as the Michelin Man. She was able to unlock a new way of seeing myself. I went on to take numerous advanced-level mathematics classes and graduated high school with academic honors. With my many challenges, I wanted to believe none of it had to do with being a Black female or trying to prove myself over my white or lighter skinned peers. It was a true fact that it had everything to do with my lack of understanding of a new curriculum in a new school district. As I was academically climbing the ladder to success, I felt the importance to establish and maintain meaningful friendships.

One of my special school friends was a Chinese boy. During down time, he taught me how to hold chopsticks, some interesting facts about Chinese culture and how challenging it was for him to not fit in. We would often exchange a shoe; I would give him my left shoe in exchange for his left shoe. We would wear each other's shoes around school and back home for a few days, and ultimately exchange them back before the weekend arrived. Not once did we ever check our race or skin tone before deciding if we would become friends first. Colorism and racism had long plagued this country; however, it seemed to be diluted or a non-factor during the shoe exchange and chopsticks experiences. During school my focus was learning, far removed from things I cared to give attention to, such as race and being light-skinned or dark-skinned. This friendship was a breath of fresh air.

My goal was to set academic and athletic aspirations, and I allowed nothing to stop me from obtaining those goals. As a result of my humble and authentic personality, academic success and athletic abilities, I quickly became a very popular person at school. At the conclusion of grade school, I had achieved exceptional honors, was a standout athlete and held leadership roles in student government and after-school clubs. I believed I had something others longed for. My Blackness was my superpower. My perfect shade of brown enveloped and secured all of my beautiful qualities. There is no question that I was aware I was a minority within the school building, but my race did not feel like a barrier. I excelled throughout high school and was excited about college. It was difficult not to make my race or skin tone an issue with all the problems I had overcome; however, it was time for the next level.

SAME YET DIFFERENT

"We all have dreams. But in order to make dreams come into reality, it takes an awful lot of determination, dedication, self-discipline, and effort." —Jesse Owens

In 1997, I attended St. Mary's College of Maryland and lived on campus. I was extremely excited about life as a college student. During my freshman year, I resided in the female dormitory with a senior class roommate. My roommate was from Ethiopia, so I must admit I was excited to have a Black roommate. Being an only child, I had never shared a room with anyone before. I had also hoped to get a glimpse of what it was like to have a sister—it did not meet my expectations. I learned that we are the same, yet different. St. Mary's College was a predominantly white, public honors college on the western shore of Maryland. I played on the women's basketball team led by a Black, female, Virginia native as the head coach.

The coach, like my math teacher, was small in stature but had the presence of a giant. Coach loved us like a mom, protected us like a dad, coached us like an MVP, challenged us like a teacher and supported us like an advocate. Coach's recruitment strategies gave several young Black women the opportunity to play basketball on a winning team at an honors college. I started freshman year as a biology major, and boy, was I stressed out. I found myself struggling just like I had done my first year in Baltimore County Schools. I shared my concerns with my coach, and she arranged time and sessions with my teacher's assistant (T.A.). After underperforming numerous times, she suggested I reevaluate my major and not hold myself to the expectations of first day registration. It had gotten to the point where school was no longer an ideal pursuit but a challenge. The high and heavy academic expectations I had set were drifting into uncharted territories. I cannot count the times I wanted to give up, but I knew giving up was the exact opposite way for me to reach my goal. Coach pushed me to continue to work hard and pursue excellence.

As academic stress began to affect my athletic performance, Coach met with me and offered me assistance and options. She also assisted me with finding work-study employment during the off season. While attending St. Mary's social groups changed. People developed friendships based on proximity to their hometown, race, and academic and athletic interests. There, all Black people knew each other as the campus was very small. Skin tone was a non-factor when race issues arouse. The Black Student Union was our hub, and a means to relay important information. After my sophomore year, I transferred to Coppin State University, a university closer to home and an HBCU (Historically Black College/University). Upon enrolling at Coppin, I took charge of my academic future, taking summer and additional courses in order to graduate ahead of schedule. I excelled exponentially in my scholarly classes. I graduated from Coppin State University magna cum laude. As I began to map out my future, I quickly discovered that a bachelor's degree in psychology did not ensure gainful employment. I knew success was on the horizon, and failure was not an option. I was career-focused and ready to capitalize on my next chapter.

LAW AND ORDER

*"Never give up, for that is just the place and time
that the tide will turn." —Harriet Beecher Stowe*

In July 2000, I joined the Police Department as a police cadet, which offered a competitive salary and much needed benefits. No one I knew could have truly prepared me for what I was about to enter into. Law enforcement is a very important and necessary occupation; without it, there is anarchy. Having educated, gay, Black females in law enforcement is both scarce and imperative. Being an educated, gay, Black female in law enforcement has unparalleled challenges, especially during the reign of the "Don't Ask, Don't Tell" era.

"Don't Ask, Don't Tell" (DADT; 1994– 2011) was the official U.S. policy on military services of non-heterosexual people, instituted during the Clinton administration. Initially, the policy was celebrated, with many believing it lifted the ban on homosexuals serving in the military. The ban had been instituted during World War II. However, a deeper look into DADT revealed that homosexuals serving in the military were not allowed to talk about their sexual orientation or engage in sexual activity, and commanding officers were not allowed to question service members about their sexual orientation. This forced service members to live in secrecy or otherwise face discharge, career loss or worse. The Police Department prides itself on being a paramilitary agency. Therefore, the example set by the federal government became an agency standard.

To be an effective law enforcement officer, one must have the ability to compartmentalize at all times and de compartmentalize once off duty. Law enforcement can impede creativity and free thinking. One must learn to primarily think critically and strategically, creating constant fight-or-flight mental scenarios and causing physical and chemical responses for things that have not and may never happen. This is compounded by the fact that at the conclusion of each fictitious scenario, you must win—or else, you will die. Law enforcement officers are trained to look for nonverbal cues to alert them of unseen danger.

Choosing to be a law enforcement officer despite the state of the nation during that time, compounded by some secret and unknown bureaucratic practices and the intense mental training of a law enforcement officer, was quite the feat to undertake for a fairly naive 20-year old, gay, Black female who believed her Blackness is magic, she was welcomed everywhere, and she could do anything as long as she put her mind to it.

Upon being sworn in, one is expected to disregard and ignore physiological responses while on duty and to get over them while off duty. Law enforcement is not about what is fair and right; it is about what is in and out of policy or what is within and against the law. The mind of a law enforcement officer is either black or white, even though the root cause of most police-related incidents is layered with multiple shades of gray. Although there is nothing wrong with black, white or gray, without warning, I learned that every uniformed and non-uniformed decision I made was being judged and evaluated by whether or not I was more Black than blue or more blue than Black by my counterparts. This was more about race than colorism. It did not matter your skin tone— what was prominent for promotions and, at times, fairness was being more white and more male.

Before being hired, I heard that my Police Agency was

the most racist police department in Maryland. Spoiler alert: After more than 20 years, I cannot confirm nor dispel that my Police Department is the most racist police department in Maryland. I can confirm, however, that there is still more work to be done within the agency, but I have met and worked with some awesome non-Black people—and a couple of pretty awful Black people. Nevertheless, during these decades of dedicated service, I would learn that all the long talks with my father about race and his Marine Corps experience would prove helpful.

Needless to say, almost every citizen interaction I've had has been under less-than-ideal circumstances. When I entered the police academy, I was the first Black female with dreadlocs. They were baby dreadlocs, but nevertheless, they were dreadlocs. The uniform policy states that an officer's hair cannot touch the collar of their uniform shirt. In order not to violate that policy, I shaved the back of my neck and kept my locs groomed weekly to uphold the uniform standards. I was later told by a Black former police training instructor that initially, my hair was a topic of discussion for a possible infraction, but he cautioned the staff not to make it an issue. My hair was never an issue during my time at the police academy. Sadly, everything else, but nothing of importance, was an issue.

I graduated from the police academy with 11 demerits, which are infractions that are documented when one does something outside of what is expected or desired, all for meaningless and highly subjective things (i.e. saying "thank you" to the uniformed senior ranking officer for holding the door for me instead of saluting said officer). On the day prior to graduation, my recruit class got a visit from representatives of the Blue Guardians, an internal organization for minorities and underrepresented members within the police department. At the conclusion of their presentation, I requested to speak with the representatives in hopes that they could help me navigate through the targeted and unfair encountered situations. I should preface this by saying the Police Department has an anti-fraternization policy. This policy restricts police recruits from fraternizing/interacting with sworn police officers while in the police academy. Regardless of the policy, I shared the challenges and treatment I experienced while in the academy. I shared about the unfair treatment and unexplained consequences for following direct orders. I shared my concern that the training staff was trying to terminate me, despite the fact that I excelled in every area of the training academy. I shared how a commanding officer pulled me into a room to tell me that he did not think police work was right for me and that he could give me a different job within the Government. Repeatedly, I refused his invitation to resign.

After I shared my experience, they requested a copy of my personnel file and had a meeting with the command staff at the training academy. Needless to say, the next day, I was sworn in and assigned to field training. Each new officer spends a two-week rotation on the road with a senior officer, also called a field training officer (FTO). My field training rotation was with a young Black man who had graduated in the class prior to mine. After driving around for some time, he pulled over and asked to speak with me outside of the police car. Outside of the police car, he informed me that I was strategically assigned to him and labeled as someone to watch closely due to a perceived inability to perform the job, with no actual justification for the label. He gave me the basic blueprint to success and encouraged me to be great, be aggressive, accept constructive criticism and cover myself. With that inside information, I was empowered to be spectacular, and I did just that.

My professional performance surpassed the supervisors' expectations. From that point on, I was able to learn various ways to handle situations. A year or so into my career, I was involved in a verbal dispute with an ex-girlfriend. Police ultimately were called due to my employment, and because it occurred in the county in which I also worked, news quickly spread that I was gay. Following the incident, I was pulled into a private meeting by two gay female commanding officers, by the way were married to each other. During that meeting, they informed me that awareness of my sexuality would pile unnecessary stress, frustration and negative attention onto me. I was also already labeled as lazy, late, argumentative and angry the day I accepted employment. One shared that Black women are disciplined harsher than white women. My sexuality increased my targeting probability. Ultimately, they suggested I hide my sexuality in an effort not to add to the list of reasons to be mishandled and mistreated. A few days later, I was approached by my male supervisor, who attempted to solicit sex from me.

After reading the police incident report, he asked, "Do you not like men at all?"

I innocently replied, "I do not hate men."

He then confessed, "I've never been with a Black woman or a lesbian before. My wife will be out of town next weekend if you are interested in coming to my house."

My 22-year-old mind did not know what to do, but I knew I was uncomfortable. Later, I shared what happened with a trusted supervisor, and he instructed me to document and report the incident. I did. When I met with the captain, she questioned what I had done to make him feel comfortable asking such a question. I was at a loss for words. *What did I do?* I did not say nor do anything to give him the impression that I was remotely interested in having sexual intercourse with him. Not long after, I was transferred to a different shift. The corporal was promoted to sergeant. Now, isn't that a bitch! In these particular situations I had encountered, one thing was for certain and two things were for sure: It had nothing to do with the tone of my skin complexion but, to my belief, it was because I was a woman, I was gay, and I was Black. All three factored into the way I was being portrayed and treated.

As I continued my career, I realized fairness is not a reality within the police department. As years passed, I watched as several Black coworkers were singled out, disciplined and terminated for incidents white officers would have received verbal counseling about. I listened as the themes of exclusion and distrust resurfaced over and over again at every precinct and unit I worked in.

I have also worked with several white male officers who have privately disclosed manufactured plans to purposely and/or intentionally exclude me from selective situations and groups. Throughout my career, despite having excellent writing and investigative skills, aggressive enforcement and minimal civilian-generated complaints, I had difficulty smoothly navigating the agency without activists, advocates and representatives helping me along the way.

As I continued through my profession, several Black women attempted to form alliances so that Black female officers could openly share their experiences and support each other. Several years into my position, I was befriended by a light-skinned female sergeant. She and another Black woman were the highest-ranking Black women in the agency. After a short friendship, I shared that I wanted to attend graduate school. She eagerly volunteered to write a letter of recommendation for me. I had also been mentored by the other Black female sergeant, who seemed to always make time for me when I had questions or concerns. Due to her heavy work schedule, she was delayed in writing my letter of recommendation for graduate school. At the 11th hour, she called and requested I pick up the letter from her residence, which was a short distance from my house. Upon picking up the letter, she provided a sealed and unsealed copy. The letter was short, sweet and to the point.

I knew that my befriended sergeant would write a detailed recommendation because that was just in her nature.

I was caught in a dilemma: Do I submit the sealed letter from my friend, or submit the short and sweet letter from my mentor? Thank God I chose my mentor's letter. Upon opening my befriended sergeant's letter, I was devastated and disappointed to find that she did not write a good letter of recommendation for me. In fact, she said she did not recommend me for graduate school because I lacked maturity. Who volunteers to write a college letter of recommendation for a friend, then does not recommend them? Colorism had reared its ugly head, and I never saw it coming. Maybe if I was light-skinned like her, I would be college material in her opinion. Her actions reminded me that evil can be displayed by the least likely source, and no one could be trusted, not even other Black women. I hated the light-skinned thoughts that quickly entered into my mind like a car racing down the highway going 100 miles per hour. Was I wrong to think it? Maybe, but I did!

MORE BLACK OR MORE BLUE

"You may not control all the events that happen to you, but you can decide not to be reduced by them."
—Maya Angelou

Throughout my line of work, I moved around the county, working in several precincts and units. I have also observed different ways communities and populations were policed. I learned that in certain parts of the county, officers are reprimanded for complaints expressed by citizens; in another area of the county, it is acceptable for officers and citizens to fight and curse each other out, then enjoy a cup of coffee the next day when everyone is sober. In another area of the county, it is not uncommon for officers to be treated like they have the plague, and citizens would rather stand outside of an open business or wait in their vehicles before crossing paths with or speaking to a uniformed police officer. There is a common experience amongst Black men and women in law enforcement. The unjustified and unaddressed instances of unfair and exclusionary practices towards Blacks, women and gays are undeniable.

In the year prior, there had been several national reports of unarmed Black men being killed at the hands of police. A senior Black commanding officer gave me a word of advice: "Don't let the title or occupation you hold prevent you from knowing who you are first."

In essence, he was saying, "You're Black first and a police officer second"; you can take off the uniform, but your skin will remain the same. In 2015, Freddie Gray died while in police custody in Baltimore City. This was the catalyst for a historical uprising in Baltimore City. I recall feeling torn about which side I should be on. On social media, my extended family and some friends were very vocal about their support of the six officers being criminally charged. I understood their position, but I knew that supporting the decision to criminally charge six police officers for his death was wrong and unjust. In that moment, I chose the side of the police. Emotions were extremely high, and the community was divided. Despite the targeted attacks orchestrated by people who wore the same uniform and took the same oath as me, I love being a police officer. I knowingly signed up for an occupation where death could be the outcome. But I can honestly say, besides one isolated incident, I have never feared that a citizen would do anything to hurt me. That feeling was not transferred to coworkers. Over time, I learned to not trust some of the people in the blue uniform. At any given moment, someone whom you have worked alongside during a critical incident will later be the person to initiate verbal or written disciplinary action. Fast forward to 2020, following the death of George Floyd—another uprising, numerous protests and violence everywhere. I chose humanity. I chose George Floyd.

As a young, unpretentious officer, I struggled to understand the difference between an officer with uncanny situational awareness and great self-defense tactics and an officer who abuses his authority with specific populations. Were they doing it right because they were better trained and had more experience, and I was doing it wrong because I was undertrained and inexperienced, or was it really an abuse of power and authority? As an experienced law enforcement officer and a gay, Black mom, I now definitively know the difference. With every single experience I have encountered throughout and during family dynamics, personal relationships, grade and high school, college, and my career, a significant amount of wisdom erupted from each, providing me a greater understanding of colorism, racism, prejudice's, biases and differences that we unconsciously and consciously invite into our lives. As a result, we must not ignore the sensitivity and importance of these racially divided complexities.

CEASE AND DESIST

"In the long run, we shape our lives, and we shape ourselves. The process never ends until we die. And the choices we make are ultimately our own responsibility." —Eleanor Roosevelt

Colorism and racism are both cancers that have infected, divided and, in some cases, destroyed family, communities and relationships. The idea that two individuals with similar education, experiences, backgrounds and abilities could be viewed as one being better than the other simply because of their skin tone is preposterous. Unfortunately, the mentality has surfaced and resurfaced over and over again within our society. An effective way to end colorism is to call it out and demand it to stop. My children will not grow up believing they are better than another simply because they are lighter-skinned than another, nor will they grow up believing they are less than enough because their skin tone is darker than a white person's. Not only is it important to talk about it—it's more important to not demonstrate or participate in it.

The mental health and wellness of our future generation is dependent on the wise to dispel the beliefs of colorism. Statistics show that in the next 20 years, Blacks and Hispanics will outnumber whites in the United States. With so many opportunities for Black excellence, skin shade exclusion will be a mere tactic for distraction by undisciplined under achievers. Moving forward, as I look ahead into the future generation to come, my hope is that I show up as I am in my beautiful brown skin. Colorism is not what I want to represent to the world. I will choose to depict a picture of hope that looks like respect from all Black and brown women worldwide. Talk is cheap; however, separating women based on their skin tone is cheaper, and I choose to be one with ALL women of color no matter the cost.

Healing and moving forward beyond the painful effects of colorism is necessary to showcase the excellence of our Blackness. As we focus on our similarities and reject the differences that divide us, we can rewrite the trajectory of our future. Every shade of brown is the true reflection of excellence and the beauty of Black women. As a beautiful black brown woman standing in the midst of colorism, I will be a model to the world that we all are the same with different amazing shades of color. Reject one of us is rejecting all of us! We will show up appearing as light, brown, darker skinned black women radiating substance and beauty. Our physical appearance will not be defined merely by our skin tone, but by representing as black women in power.

DR. SHONEIKA MOORE, 35

Being in love with helping people can leave you looking back at how you missed the opportunity to help yourself. Dr. Shoneika Moore grew up in Harlem, New York, and had a child at the age of 16. Shortly after that, she decided to drop out of high school to go after things that she would later find out had lesser value. Struggling to find happiness while in brokenness, she took some wrong paths. She became a single mother who strived to better herself against all odds while trying to take others with her.

We all go through many things in life, but the goal is to overcome them. We grow by not letting the negative issues we go through break us and learning to make our mess a message. We were all created for God's purpose to be different, stand out and produce fruit of His work.

Dr. Moore's passion has always been to help others and guide them to see the true beauty of brokenness. We all have the keys to unlock the doors God has provided for us. During her journey, Dr. Moore realized that everyone can't handle change, and some want to stay where they are. She didn't get discouraged; she decided to walk in her full potential and allow God to bring her to those whom she needed to help. Dr. Shoneika Moore was called to a special group of people. They are people who are determined to overcome, change, and live better, all for God's purpose!

Dr. Moore graduated with a bachelor of science in business marketing and completed seminary school, where she received her Ph.D. in theology at Bible Institutes of America along with other certifications. Dr. Moore is very involved in her community in Wilmington, Delaware, where she formed the children's mentor group "Secure The Seed," aimed to mold youth into the leaders they are called to be. Shoneika is a caring mother of four talented children—Chauncey, Cetra, Wynter & Lj—and strives to see a change in the community, starting with children.

Certified Master Power Coach | Author| International Speaker

DEDICATION

My chapter of the book is dedicated to moms who raised children with different skin tones because they might have had different fathers, or somewhere down the blood line, a relative popped up and changed things. It's not easy knowing that your children are siblings, yet people treat them differently. I've watched it with my own eyes, and God bless my children who have been so blind to the fact that it was going on.

My daughters Cetra and Wynter both come from me, but Wynter is bi racial and lighter, and Cetra is darker. Both of my girls are beautiful and unique in their own way. I sat back for years watching the difference in treatment as my own study, and then I got to write about it years later. God always has a plan for everything you do when you don't know why you're doing something. Instead of verbally correcting people, my actions would show in how I wanted my baby girls to be treated. They have blossomed so well because I needed to make sure they didn't experience what I went through as a kid.

There are a lot of parents who don't talk about it and just normalize it like I almost did. I saw favoritism between them, and I nipped it right away with anyone who tried it. They have an age difference: one is 15 and the other is 12. They have managed to not help me with this chapter of mine by having no experiences of their own. When I heard that, I realized the seeds I was planting grew and will continue to grow as they get older. No child should have to go through being treated differently because of the color of their skin.

We are all beautiful no matter the shade, and we are ENOUGH the way we are... Shine, Black and brown girls. Shine.

CONNECT WITH SHONEIKA

Facebook: Shoneika Moore
Twitter: Shoneika Moore
YouTube: Shoneika Moore
Instagram: NeikaSpeaks
TikTok: NeikaSpeaks

COLORS

Every time I look back at a childhood picture, I admire how cutely my mother dressed me— how nice my hair was and how whatever I was wearing, the bobos and berets matched to a T. You couldn't tell me nothing until I realized that my skin color wasn't ideal. What looked pretty to me wasn't pretty to others. People don't realize that depression starts at an early age with children, fighting to belong when you're so small in a big world.

Daycare and school were the worst! I felt like I was being bullied in every area of my life. At home, I felt like my mother didn't like me for some strange reason because I stayed getting my ass beat. Then, when I went to school, ready to get away from home, it was like a color war zone. The pretty girls were always deemed the "light-skinned girls," and the "dark-skinned girls" were the so-called ugly ones. It didn't help that I used to travel down South for the summers, so I would always come back darker than what I was before I left.

When I went away to camp, it was the same thing. I was always "the Black girl." I struggled a lot because I wanted to be lighter. I hated getting teased. I would get called names like "Blackie"; then, when I would come back from camp or the South, I'm not sure what the sun did to me, but I always was darker on one side of my face than the other. The kids started calling me "two-faced." I really couldn't win. I started to hate going to school and hate my skin. I wanted to be lighter and even started looking into how to be lighter. Can you imagine a child looking into how to bleach their skin? I wanted straight, long hair, bigger boobs and a music video body. All over the TV, you would see light-skinned girls with nice bodies.

No child should have all of that on their mind, and it scared me when I started raising children because if I was like that as a child, I could only imagine what the kids today are going through with all this social media. It wasn't until 1999, when TLC's music video for "Unpretty" came out, that I snapped out of not loving myself. I was only 11 years old, and I wanted to make all these life changes. That video was a big inspiration and showed the things that people go through when they want to be someone else. It scared me— I know that!

COLORISM

"Look to a day when people will not be judged by the color of their skin." —Martin Luther King Jr.

Colorism is prejudice or discrimination against a dark skin tone, typically among people of the same ethnic or racial group (Definitions from Oxford Languages).

Colorism is a form of discrimination or prejudice in which people are treated differently based on the shade or tone of their skin color, typically favoring lighter skin tones over darker ones. This bias or discrimination often occurs within racial or ethnic groups and can manifest in various ways, including social, economic and political contexts.

Colorism has deep historical roots, often stemming from the legacy of colonialism, slavery and imperialism. European colonial powers frequently favored individuals with lighter skin, and this preference continued in post-colonial societies.

Colorism can have profound effects on individuals, influencing their self-esteem, self-worth and opportunities in life. People with darker skin tones may face disadvantages in education, employment and social interactions.

It is important to understand that colorism is a complex and deeply ingrained issue, and addressing it requires both individual awareness and systemic change. Promoting inclusivity, embracing diversity and challenging beauty standards that perpetuate colorism are essential steps toward combatting this form of discrimination.

HOW SKIN TONES HAVE AFFECTED YOUR LIFE

"Imagine hating a complete stranger because their skin tone is lighter or darker than yours." —Wayne Gerard Trotman

I didn't like the skin I was in. I felt like all the lighter people got so much respect and were favored. They were always called pretty, always got the attention and always had the boys all over them. I wanted attention, I wanted to feel loved and I wanted to feel like people liked me. The older I became, I did anything for attention— how I dressed and how I acted, and when it came to dressing, I loved bright, "can't miss her" colors. I wanted to make sure I stood out.

Guess what ... When I did do that, I started hearing, "You're pretty for a dark-skinned girl," and that just made me angry. I couldn't stand the fact that people really ignored dark-skinned girls. Why do I have to overcompensate just to get attention? I really turned into an angry, disrespectful kid. I was dealing with physical abuse at home, I was not the right color outside of my house, my father was in prison, I dealt with incest on both sides of the family and mentally, I tied it all together and thought all this was happening because I was too dark. When you turned on the TV, most of the women who were raped were dark. Very few movies had a light-skinned girl getting violated.

I really felt like I had something to prove. I was always

ready to fight and had a nasty attitude because I wanted people to see how dark-skinned chicks get down, but I went the wrong way about it now that I look at it. I really wish my younger self could have talked about it because I was so broken inside and turned to things that didn't help. I wanted to see how many guys I could pull with my looks, how many cool people I could hang out with. The crazy part about all this is that the dark-skinned girls didn't like me. So, I was really confused.

Skin tone can influence how individuals perceive themselves and how they are perceived by others. It can shape one's cultural and racial identity, affecting their sense of belonging within a particular community.

HOW YOU FEEL ABOUT BEING A BLACK WOMAN IN BROWN SKIN

"I'm convinced that we Black women possess a special indestructible strength that allows us to not only get down, but to get up, to get through, and to get over." —Janet Jackson

Being a Black woman with brown skin may mean different things to different people, as experiences and perceptions can vary widely. It can involve a sense of pride in one's cultural heritage and identity, as well as an awareness of the challenges and discrimination that can come with being part of a marginalized group. It can also be a source of strength, resilience and empowerment, as many Black women with brown skin have played significant roles in history, culture, and social movements.

It took me years to embrace being a Black woman in brown skin. I wanted to be lighter for so long because I thought lighter-skinned women got more respect. It seemed like they got the world handed to them, while brown, darker-skinned women had to work ten times harder. On TV, it looked that way, and it definitely felt that way while I grew up, starting in school. Teachers would always play favoritism to the light-skinned kids. It seemed like that they got the best grades and the best seats in the class, they were always up under the teacher and their punishment never added up if they did something wrong.

As a child, people will try to make you think you're tripping, like you don't see what you are seeing. That's exactly what happened to me. I was very outspoken and still am today, but when I said something about things being and looking different, I would always get in trouble. It was almost like a "suppress dark girls" movement. Take their voice and separate them— it was definitely an agenda. I watched a lot of talk shows, and there was nothing but white or light-skinned women, mainly white. When I finally saw Oprah, I knew that I had a chance, and one day, I would have a TV show just like her. I never really paid attention to the topics; I was just so mesmerized at the fact that a brown girl did it.

I really looked up to that and always said I would meet Oprah one day and sit on her couch. I was also inspired the older I got when Black History Month came around. Although I felt like we deserved more than February, that was the one month in a year I looked forward to as a child. I would get on my computer and look up Black women who did something in the world. This played a major part in my self-esteem, but I still questioned why more people didn't know and why it was like the Black (darker) women who really did something in the world were hidden.

Elizabeth Freeman: Also known as Mumbet or Bet, she was the first African American woman slave to successfully file a lawsuit in Massachusetts for freedom and won.

Harriet Tubman: She was known as "Moses of her people"; she was enslaved, escaped and helped others gain their freedom as a conductor of the Underground Railroad. I had the pleasure of playing her in my elementary school play.

Ida B. Wells: She was a prominent Black investigative journalist, educator and activist in the early civil rights movement. She was one of the founders of the NAACP (National Association for the Advancement of Colored People) and led a powerful anti-lynching crusade in the U.S. in the 1890s.

Mya Angelou: She was a Black writer and activist. Her legacy included a well-known body of work with her memoirs, poems, essays and plays. In 1969, she became famous after her publication I Know Why the Caged Bird Sings, an autobarotropy detailing her early years as a young Black woman.

Wangari Maathai: She was the first Black African woman to receive a Nobel Peace Prize for her efforts in environmental conservation. In the 1970s, she founded the Green Belt Movement, an environmental non-governmental organization focused on environmental conservation and women's rights. She was also an elected member of Parliament and served as assistant minister for Environment and Natural Resources.

Ruby Bridges: She was an American activist who helped the civil rights movement in Louisiana. She was the first child to desegregate William Frantz Elementary School, an all-white school in Louisiana, which she was selected to attend based on her displayed intelligence at just six years old. She also was later painted by Norman Rockwell and is now celebrated as a courageous Black woman who continued to fight for equal rights throughout her life.

Madam C. J. Walker: She was an African American entrepreneur, philanthropist and political and social activist. She is recorded as the first female self-made millionaire in America in the Guinness Book of World Records with her hair care line.

Valerie L. Thomas: She is an American data scientist and inventor. She invented the illusion transmitter, for which she received a patent in 1980. She was responsible for developing the digital media formats that image processing systems used in the early years of NASA's Landsat program.

Oprah Gail Winfrey: She is an American talk show host,

television producer, actress, author and media proprietor. She is best known for her talk show, The Oprah Winfrey Show, broadcast from Chicago, which ran in national syndication for 25 years, from 1986 to 2011.

I wanted to be like every one of them. Every career day, Halloween, etc., if we had to dress up, I was a Black businesswoman. I would put on my baby blue two-piece skirt suit with my white shoes and walk around the school with my briefcase. When people would ask, I would simply say I'm a businesswoman. I felt like if nobody else did, I would start at a young age. I was very determined as a child to change things for my age group. A lot of highlighted women when I was growing up were biracial, and you really had to dig for some of the dark-skinned women who did something in the world.

PRIVILEGES WITHIN THE BLACK COMMUNITY: LIGHTER-SKINNED WOMEN/PEOPLE

"The black skin is not a badge of shame, but rather a glorious symbol of national greatness." —Marcus Garvey

Privilege within the Black community based on skin tone is a complex and sensitive issue, often referred to as "colorism." Colorism is a form of discrimination or bias that favors individuals with lighter skin tones over those with darker skin tones, and it can be found within many racial and ethnic communities— definitely the Black community. It's important to understand that privilege based on skin tone is a social construct and does not have a basis in biology or inherent worth. People have created this separation amongst one another, and it has been passed down from generation to generation.

Colorism has deep historical roots, dating back to slavery and colonialism. Lighter-skinned slaves were often given preferential treatment by their oppressors, which contributed to the perpetuation of colorism within the Black community. In most cases, individuals with lighter skin may have economic and social advantages within the Black community. They may face less discrimination and bias, have easier access to certain resources and experience fewer stereotypes.

Colorism can and has had harmful consequences, including perpetuating divisions within the Black community, reinforcing harmful beauty standards and negatively affecting individuals' self-esteem and mental health. I was a victim of these consequences growing up. I didn't think I was good enough being dark. I would always try to out do the next chick by wearing bright colors to be more fashionable and get noticed as a dark-skinned bBlack girl who would grow into a woman. People don't really understand how that can play with your mental health.

Not thinking you're good enough because you have darker skin makes you want to go crazy. Although your skin color has nothing to do with you, you start to question everything. Would I have more friends if I was lighter? Would more people like me if I was lighter? Would I have more money if I was lighter? Would I get more business deals if I was lighter? aAnd the list goes on. On top of life itself, this is too much to be thinking about all the time. When you have bills building, and if— God forbid— you have children, you're taking care of them either as a single mother, co-parenting or in a relationship, you have a lot on your plate. Then, you come home and are left with your thoughts: Would the outcome have changed if...

There's a lot to deal with, and I had to tell myself every time something didn't work out quite right, "L et's not think it's the color of your skin." That's a bad space to be in. Coaching yourself out of a stigma can cause depression— and depressed I was.

MEDIA AND REPRESENTATION

*"Whoever controls the media, the images, controls
the culture." —Allen Ginsberg*

The media has played a significant role in perpetuating colorism by often promoting lighter-skinned individuals as more desirable and successful. This can lead to greater opportunities and representation in various industries for those with lighter skin tones. Media often perpetuates Eurocentric beauty standards, where lighter skin is considered more beautiful and desirable. This can be seen in casting choices, advertising and the portrayal of characters in movies, TV shows and advertisements.

Dark-skinned individuals, especially women, have historically been underrepresented in leading roles and positive character portrayals. Lighter-skinned actors and actresses are often favored in casting decisions, reinforcing colorist attitudes. They stereotype darker-skinned characters and sometimes typecast them into specific roles, often as villains, criminals or low-status individuals. These portrayals contribute to negative stereotypes and reinforce biases. Some celebrities and individuals in the public eye resort to skin-lightening practices to conform to these beauty standards, sending harmful messages to their audiences and perpetuating colorism.

Constant exposure to these biased portrayals can lead to lower self-esteem and self-worth among people with darker skin tones. It can also contribute to a sense of marginalization and exclusion. Social media has played a significant role in raising awareness about colorism and holding media outlets accountable for their portrayals. Activists and influencers have used their platforms to challenge harmful narratives and promote self-love and acceptance.

Slowly but surely, things are moving towards more diversity, but it's still a fight. It's still a fight in homes, schools, the workplace, what you see on TV, social media and, most of all, in your mind. I'm 35 years old, and sometimes, I still struggle with the thoughts. I've seen celebrities who I love to bleach their skin just to fit in in the industry. So, when people with money are doing it, you start to battle with yourself no matter how positive you try to be.

When it comes down to it, going back to the root is always important. Speaking to that inner child and freeing that person is a healing journey like no other. No matter what contamination goes on around us, we must know the TRUTH that no matter what skin tone, no matter how we used it in the past for good or bad, WE ARE ENOUGH.

I might be dark-skinned...
I'M ENOUGH.
I might look different from what's in the media...
I'M ENOUGH.
My childhood might not have been perfect...
I'M ENOUGH.
My process might be slower...
I'M ENOUGH.
My future is as bright as I want it to be because...
I'M ENOUGH

One of my favorite poems growing up as a child helped me remember that although I'm BLACK, I can be what I want to be.

HEY, BLACK CHILD
WRITTEN BY USENI EUGENE PERKINS

Hey, Black Child
Do you know who you are
Who you really are
Do you know you can be
What you want to be
If you try to be
What you can be

Hey, Black Child
Do you know who you are
Where you're really going
Do you know you can learn
What you want to learn
What you can learn

Hey, Black Child
Do you know you are strong
I mean really strong
Do you know you can do
What you want to do
If you try to do
What you can do

Hey, Black Child
Be what you can be
Learn what you must learn
Do what you can do
And tomorrow, your nation
Will be what you want it to be

The effects of colorism in childhood can persist into adulthood, impacting one's relationships, career and overall quality of life. It can create a cycle of discrimination that is passed down from one generation to the next, which can have a long-term impact. Like I stated, I over compensated for years because I had low self-esteem from being too dark. Today, you can't tell me nothing. I did the deep work and uprooted ways of thinking I had in the past and took on a bold approach. God isn't a liar, so He made me this way for a reason. He gave me a unique situation in my household for a reason.

To all my chocolate girls (that's what they call me), you are who God created you to be. You are beautiful in the shade He made you. Nobody can take away your uniqueness, so embrace it, own it and walk in it!

I AM ENOUGH!

ALEXIS TERRY, 26

Alexis Terry is a writer, perpetual seeker of knowledge, and a staunch advocate for individuals with marginalized identities. She holds a degree in Mass Communications and Women and Gender Studies from Towson University, as well as a Masters degree in Human Resource Development from Villanova University.

Currently residing in Baltimore City with her beloved cat Harriet. Furthermore, her professional endeavors in the ed-tech industry revolve around cultivating learning and development opportunities, leaving an indelible impact on individuals' growth and empowerment. Alongside her professional pursuits, she finds joy in spending time with loved ones, exploring new music, and actively volunteering.

"Women of Color" marks Alexis' debut as a published author, encompassing her multifaceted journey and embodying her distinctive perspective. She invites you on an enthralling exploration of triumph, resilience, and the vibrant tapestry of her experiences.

ACKNOWLEDGMENT

Mom, without you there would be no me. Thank you from the depths of my heart for everything you've done for me.

Joseph, my little brother, it's us against the world. Forever.

My grandma Wilma, "Maw"—the blueprint truly. Thank you for paving the way.

The homies, my forever friends, thank you for loving and supporting me beyond measure.

DEDICATION

This is for you, Dad. I miss you every day. I can't wait to see you again.

A NOTE

*"I am not free while any woman is unfree, even when
her shackles are very different from my own."*
—Audre Lorde

As I began writing for this book, I was adamant that my story wouldn't revolve around the suffering of a light-skinned person or solely represent the Black experience. I even questioned if my experience mattered and if it was worth sharing. Yes, the identity struggle of being light skinned is real and painful but it's not in comparison to the pain of being systemically harmed because of the pigmented color of your skin. Yet, I've reached a conclusion: This is *my* experience. We are all shaped by our lived experiences, and this is mine—a journey entangled in the roots of white supremacy and Black liberation. I believe I was placed on this Earth to utilize my privilege in working alongside my brothers and sisters to bridge the gap that colorism has created. Together, we can build trust, dismantle the walls of anger and hostility, and extend our full hearts to one another.

WHO AM I?

I wrestle with my identity... not the one I created for myself, but the one that people created for me.

I am a walking contradiction, a puzzle for others to solve.

I'm either too Black or my melanin is too far dissolved.

I am a blend of cultures, a mixture of different hues and sometimes I swear I feel like I don't belong to either of the two.

I walk into a room and I'm crowned the pretty lightskin girl with good hair, left with the feeling that something about me doesn't belong there.

I walk into the other room and they're too stunned to speak. In this room, my Blackness is not seen as a defeat. Someone utters the words "you're so pretty for a Black girl"

Why can't I just be seen for being me?

HOW WOULD THE WORLD VIEW ME?

"I define myself. My identity is mine to create, not the world's to dictate." —Angela Davis

My dad was Black, and my mom is a mix of European ethnicities. She has always simply referred to herself as a white woman and I've always referred to myself as "mixed". I don't consider myself to be white passing, but my ethnic ambiguity allows me to pass as something else. I'm unsure of my mothers origins, as she was adopted as a baby and the closest thing I have to understanding where she came from is 23andMe results. Anyway, on June 20th, 1997. I entered the world as a light skin baby to no one's surprise. There are times that I wonder if my parents thought about the complexities of raising a mixed kid in America? Was my white mom prepared to raise a little Black girl? Would I be fully accepted by my extended white family that had a history of racist and prejudiced behavior? Would my darker skinned family members and friends trust that I was "one of them" despite our skintone being on the opposite sides of the spectrum?

Tyler, The Creator said it best, "I'm a fucking walking paradox." My light skin is beautiful and not ethnically legitimate.

Growing up, I was taught to embrace my Blackness with pride. However, I remained oblivious to how my light skin unwittingly perpetuated systems of racial oppression. I believed my experiences aligned with those of my Black peers, regardless of our skin tones. My circle consisted of Black friends, my skin bore a tint, I religiously styled my hair in cornrows, I kept up with the slang and I saw myself reflected in Black culture.

I can vividly recollect instances when I received extra attention simply because of the combination of having lighter skin, looser curls, and what some might describe as pretty eyes. I distinctly recall an unsettling incident when someone made a comment insinuating that, had I lived in a different time, I might have been consigned to a life of servitude indoors. It was a jarring moment, yet strangely, it didn't immediately register to me the existence of systemic privilege for those who share my appearance. You see, during my early years in grade school, the topic of slavery was presented in a way that oversimplified its complexities, as if it were a "one size fits all" narrative. They failed to delve into the intricacies of racism, opting instead for a starkly binary portrayal. It was only as I journeyed through life that I began to grasp the nuances and layers of this issue, leading to a profound shift in my understanding.

As I got older and moved into more racially and economically diverse areas, I started to feel like I didn't fit in anywhere. I was too black for the white kids and too white for the black kids. It's then that I started to realize how the world viewed me.

We know Imposter Syndrome as a psychological occurrence in which an individual doubts their skills, talents, or accomplishments and has a persistent internalized fear of being exposed as a fraud. In America, being mixed race has left me with a sense of imposter syndrome. Picture it as if I were engaged in a never-ending sports game, where one player continually draws penalty flags. However, in my case, these flags are not related to sports but rather pertain to my identity – always judged as being too much of one thing or too little of another. It's a perpetual balancing act, striving to navigate the complexities of my mixed heritage in a society that often insists on assigning rigid labels and expectations based on appearance and background.

I went to live with my grandma in Shrewsbury, PA during middle school because the school system was better than the city schools I was previously attending. In this small town, the number of Black people could be counted on just a couple of hands, and I found myself in a situation where I had transitioned from an environment predominantly composed of Black and Hispanic peers to one where I often stood out as the sole Black student in the classroom. It was nothing short of a culture shock. However, over time I worked hard to better blend in with those around me. My braids and curls quickly turned into heat damaged straight hair. I started doing weird things like wearing Monster shirts and obsessing over white boy bands.

During this period, my evolving understanding of racism and how to navigate predominantly white spaces seemed to point me in one clear direction: earn the favor of white people. It became evident to me that white individuals often had the discretion to select which Black individuals were deemed acceptable for friendship. So, I made it my mission to do everything in my power to gain their approval. I meticulously crafted my interests and preferences to align with theirs, and I went to great lengths to assimilate, striving to adopt the appearance and mannerisms that would make me resemble a white person as closely as possible. I already had the lightskin, my actions had to prove it. In my pursuit to fit in and be accepted, I believed I was doing all the right things, convinced that by sharing their likes and striving to mirror their cultural identity, I could bridge the gap that seemed to divide us.

It's difficult to admit these things because, deep down,

I have always cherished my Black identity. Being white was never something I proudly proclaimed from the rooftops, except when it offered the potential to gain entry into spaces where I might otherwise be ignored. However, a profound internal struggle began when I was forced to demonstrate my authenticity as a Black person or prove my worthiness in a community I cherished and had no intention of causing harm to.

I can still recall the overwhelming waves of shame, guilt, and embarrassment that washed over me. How could I have been so naive and turned a blind eye to the mistreatment of my darker-skinned sisters, while placing individuals with lighter skin, like myself, on a pedestal? These feelings were the catalyst for a deeper exploration of my own identity, a quest for self-acceptance, and a commitment to finding my place within a community I loved, all while reckoning with the privilege and biases that had shaped my perspective for far too long.

A lot of life has happened between now and then, that was over 10 years ago. I embrace my curly hair now – that is not to say I won't get me a silk press but I don't feel like I need a silk press. I don't *need* white people's approval anymore.

I was at a bar recently and there was a dark skinned Black woman crying and getting sick in the bathroom. I think we were the only Black identifying people in the whole establishment. I offered my help to her, she accepted, and I followed up with a "Us Black women have to stick together, it's hard out here." I don't know if I said this because it's true or because I drank too much tequila and was saying anything at this point, but I wanted her to know she was safe with me. She turns to me and says, "But you don't really know." Confused with a crinkle in my eyebrow, I asked her "what do you mean?" she looked me dead in my face and said "you are light skin, you don't know what it's like." I took a step back, hand on my heart because it felt like she stabbed me, caught my breath, and replied, "you're right." I don't remember much after that besides my friend meeting me at the bathroom door with an espresso martini. I chugged it. I think about this moment a lot and it's one of the few moments I can remember from that night. It has become a strong reflection point for me as I learn to navigate spaces as a light skinned person of color.

While I did take it personally for a moment, I can't blame her for not trusting me and it wasn't necessarily about *me*. Colorism operates as an arm of racism giving me and others light skin privilege. We hold more power than is just. We unproportionately have more access across the board and we continue to not share or give up space. This is only a problem that lighter skinned people can fix by taking a step back, lifting while we climb and making space for Black people.

YOU

To my sisters of ebony, strong and bold.

I give you my hand, I see you as whole.

Your beauty is a testament to all that we possess.

I hate that the world has viewed you as less.

I will amplify your voice

I won't dim your light

And I promise to stand with you through the fight.

MENTAL HEALTH

"Taking care of your mind is not a sign of weakness but a testament to your strength." —Gabby Douglas

Mental Health was something that was never talked about much in my family until the more recent years of my life and I attribute that to the increased access to education and healthcare amongst the younger generations. There were never talks of therapy, medications, and treatments and if there were, it was a secret to be kept. I think I can speak for others here when I say that there is a strong stigma around mental health in the Black community dating back to the days of slavery.

The first time I saw a therapist, I was 15 years old and my dad had just died a year before. My school counselor at the time recommended I see a therapist after I had a panic attack at school. When I was experiencing this panic attack, I didn't understand what was happening to me. I was having trouble breathing, nauseous, confused and my body's emotions felt ready to implode. I remember going to the nurses office and (with an attitude) they sent me to the counseling office. I didn't understand why I was being sent there because at the time I didn't know how panic and anxiety displayed itself. No one ever told me because instead they were telling me I would be okay. The counseling office was always packed with black students and now I know why...it was the only place where our emotions were taken seriously and our voices were heard.

My therapy journey began, but I soon found myself grappling with a sentiment shared by many who came before me: a reluctance to confide my innermost thoughts to a white therapist. Anxiety persisted within me. The following year, another severe panic attack struck, leading to my prescription of a selective serotonin reuptake inhibitor (SSRI) to manage my anxiety and depression. Despite this intervention, my understanding of my own condition remained incomplete. I harbored frustration towards myself for my perceived inability to function. Depression began to cast its heavy shadow, fueled by self-loathing, the void left by my departed father, and an ever-present desire to escape the pain of existence.

10 years later, I still struggle with my mental health but it looks a lot different now. During college, life got weird again. I was in my first serious relationship, someone close to me was battling addiction, I was broke, stressed and unhealthy. The anxiety attacks started again, my grades started slipping and I lost over 25 pounds. I was hurting...bad. After confiding in friends and professors, I went to the counseling center and scheduled an appointment with an on campus therapist. I felt so much relief just scheduling the appointment. Eventually, I was placed with a therapist external to the university. He has been my therapist on and off for 6 years now. I've learned so much, it has not been easy but the work has been far worth the reward. I am able to recognize when my soul is not aligned and I now have techniques that bring me back to Earth when the only thing I want to do is float away into the universe.

The other day I expressed to my therapist that I was struggling with expressing my emotions, those good and bad but especially the bad ones and I happened to also share that I am writing about my experience as a Black woman for this book. We talked for a bit and he said, "Well...aren't you doing what the world expects out of a Black woman?" The Strong Black Woman is immune to obstacles and pain. If I didn't just push things aside and keep grinding I would be considered weak to the world. We are suffering from the "Strong Black Woman" cultural trope that has left us burnout, suffering in silence and physically ill. How can they expect so little from Black people and so much at the same time?

Most recently I was diagnosed with ADHD. One of the forms I had to fill out allowed me to rank areas of behavior from elementary school. Once I was finished I realized I had been showing the signs all along and it is now becoming a disruption in my everyday life. I reflected for a while wondering if anyone else noticed these things when I was younger. I realized my consistent chattiness in class and inability to raise my hand were all viewed as personality issues at school and behavioral issues at home that could be fixed with a punishment of some sorts. I suspect that it was easy for my teachers to write these things off as personality traits because of my lightskin, whereas my darker skinned classmates were getting written up left and right. The only time this looked different in life was during middle school in Shrewsbury. Despite my light hue, I was seen as a Black kid with behavioral issues and my white peers were now the kids with exuberant personalities.

My dad always told me that no matter how light I am, when push comes to shove, white people will still only see my Blackness. I grew up thinking that ADHD was not a real thing and my peers just needed a spanking and didn't listen to instructions. I definitely didn't think I could have ADHD, there was no way. I actually thought it was a white people thing because due to the stigmas of mental health in the black community, black children were never getting diagnosed and medicated, instead we were getting in trouble at home and told to stop acting stupid at school. Getting an ADHD diagnosis and being properly medicated has been one of the best things that has ever happened to me. I can keep my room cleaned and organized, I can get my work done in a timely manner and not rush at the last minute, I can remember daily tasks and overall my quality of life has improved for the better.

My mental health journey now in my life is about not letting me push myself to no return. It's unlearning the behaviors that have been ingrained in my brain to continue working and stressing past exhaustion because I've made being a strong black woman a part of my identity. Don't get me wrong, I love being strong and resilient and I would also enjoy a life of ease, patience, saying no and having the courage to be vulnerable. This pressure along with the marginalization and oppression that black women endure is enough to take someone out...for good. I am a work in progress. My mental health continues to be a battle and I will win. I do my best to set aside these stigmas and categorizations based on the color of my skin. I seek help when I need it and I am on a journey to be my best self. I look back at my 16 year old self and I want to embrace her with a hug and teach her all of the things I've learned.

Take care of yourself, get a mental health professional and start healing now, it's never too late and you don't have to do this on your own.

If you or someone you know is experiencing a mental health or substance use crisis, call or text 988.

DEAR BLACK BEAUTIFUL QUEENS,

Hey, you—yes, you, with your black and brown, bold, driven, empowered, exceptional, fierce, independent and tenacious selves. I know you might have questioned who you were, why you existed, or if you mattered. Let me help you out: YES, ALL OF YOU MATTER... Every part of your existence is divine, your smile is bright, your curves are just right. Trust me—you ALL are inspiring and radiating queens!

Walk in your power. Show up and be confident. Speak your truth. Do not deny your strength. Trust in your abilities to WIN. Be free and liberating. Be the tallest in every room you enter. You are chosen, loved, optimistic, special and stunning. *YOU ARE A MIRACLE. YOU ARE PERFECT JUST THE WAY YOU ARE. HUG AND EMBRACE YOURSELF. WE LOVE YOU, QUEENS, AND WE ARE BLACK GIRL MAGIC FOR LIFE!!*

WE ARE GORGEOUS BLACK WOMEN. LET'S UNIFY AND BE THE CHANGE THAT'S LONG OVERDUE. WE HAVE BEEN DIVIDED LONG ENOUGH!! WE HAVE FACED MANY CHALLENGES; NOW, IT IS TIME TO OVERCOME. THERE ARE NO LIMITATIONS! LET US USE OUR PAIN AND TRAUMA TO CHANGE THE WORLD!

"I need to see my own beauty and continue to be reminded that I am enough, that I am worthy of love without effort, that I am beautiful, that the texture of my hair and that the shape of my curves, the size of my lips, the color of my skin, and the feelings that I have are all worthy and okay."
— *Tracee Ellis Ross*

Love, Your Black Sister Queens,
Alexis, Felicia, Juanika, Monica, Sharron and Shoneika...

www.ingramcontent.com/pod-product-compliance
Lightning Source LLC
Chambersburg PA
CBHW051246020426

42333CB00025B/3075